A Barna Report
Produced in Partnership
with Alpha USA

REVIVING EVANGELISM

Current Realities That
Demand a New Vision for
Sharing Faith

ISBN: 978-1-945269-33-2

Funding for this research was made possible by the generous support of Alpha USA. Barna Group was solely responsible for data collection, analysis and writing of the report.

CONTENTS

PREFACE

By Craig Springer

Executive Director of Alpha USA

You've heard the evangelism analogy before: If you go to a fantastic restaurant or watch an unforgettable movie, what's the first thing you want to do after you savor the moment? Share it! You want to tell someone about the wagyu beef or bacon-wrapped dates or kale salad surprise (if that's your thing). It's natural to want others to experience what we love. Unfortunately, when it comes to evangelism in America, this instinct is fading fast. We post Instagram novellas of what we had for dinner but, in an interesting twist of our time, U.S. Christians are losing a desire to share their faith.

Why is this happening? Before we resort to Millennial shaming, angry preaching or incessant training courses, we need to understand what is going on. Is there an increase in self-centeredness, a decrease in authentic spiritual experiences, a lack of teaching on evangelism in our churches? Are our methods to train and send Christians into the world faulty or dated? Our drive to understand *why* is what inspired Alpha USA to commission this project.

Once we understand the *why*, then we can get to the *what*. What needs to change so we can buck the trend and meaningfully share the love and truth of Jesus in a country where he is desperately needed? Because Romans 10:14 remains as true as it has ever been: "How can they believe in him if they have never heard about him? And how can they hear about him unless someone tells them?"

Without giving you a full spoiler, here is a bit of what you are in for: Some of the findings in this report will surprise you, some will downright break your heart, some are deeply insightful and some provide practical direction for how we can adjust our personal evangelism and evangelism training strategies in our churches.

At Alpha, we've been wrestling for decades with many of the questions embedded in this monograph. Alpha began some 30 years ago at Holy Trinity Brompton Church (HTB) in London.

At the time, it seemed clear that people were not responding to traditional methods of evangelism and that trust in the Church and in Christianity, as a whole, was diminishing—while skepticism was on the rise. Instead of Christian proclamation, HTB believed that people were hungering for open-ended conversation without any arm-twisting and confrontational correction. So, the church's leaders tried something new. They began inviting people outside of the church to a meal, welcoming them as they were, giving a short, unassuming talk on faith and then, during group discussion, listening more than speaking. Word spread and over time hundreds and then thousands of people began showing up to explore Jesus in central London through the Alpha program.

When Alpha began, it was in an environment where the pursuit of faith, the effectiveness of the Church and trust in the Bible had slipped away in a multicultural, post-Christian city center. People were no longer listening to the Church, and Christians were sharing their faith less and less. In many ways, the trends facing Western Europe then foreshadowed the realities we now see in the United States.

Christians in America are losing a desire to share thier faith

As a pastor for many years, I saw the trends of declining effectiveness in evangelism play out over time. We did everything we could to change this—poured money into better weekend programs, ran thousands of people through classes on how to share their faith, preached our socks off on the importance of the call to evangelize—yet we didn't see any major ongoing shift or sustained spiritual fruit in the face of our changing culture.

So when I discovered Alpha's impact in the post-Christian environment of London, I got interested. We implemented Alpha over time and began to see the direction of the trends shift. More non-Christians were coming to our church and developing a relationship with Jesus. Christians were more emboldened and equipped to invite their friends to explore Jesus. A nucleus of impassioned Christ-followers were praying with intention and seeing the spiritual fruit of lives changed before their eyes. This began to change our church and buck the declining evangelism trend.

Alpha USA commissioned this study to discover what it will take to revive evangelism across the United States. We long for the day when every Christian of every generation is empowered to share Jesus, when every church is growing in its impact in their community and millions more say yes to Christ. Our dream is nothing less than the awakening of the American Church. Although the statistics of a quieted and declining Christian community are startling, the opportunity is now and the generation who can lead the charge is right here in our midst. We are, all together, part of the larger story of what God is doing to bring renewal to our communities and revitalization to his Church.

Let's learn together what it will take to see an awakening in our day. ✳

DEFINITIONS

- **Practicing Christians** identify as Christian, agree strongly that faith is very important in their lives and have attended church within the past month.

- **All others** are US adults who are not practicing Christians under the definition above. These fall into two main groups:

  - **Lapsed Christians** identify as Christian but have not attended church within the past month. Only 4 percent consider their faith very important.

  - **Non-Christians** identify with a faith other than Christianity ("religious non-Christians") or with no faith at all ("atheists / agnostics / nones").

- **Millennials** were born 1984 to 1998 (ages 20 to 34).

- **Gen X** were born 1965 to 1983 (ages 35 to 53).

- **Boomers** were born 1946 to 1964 (ages 54 to 72).

- **Elders** were born before 1946 (age 73+).

KEY FINDINGS AMONG PRACTICING CHRISTIANS

Nearly half of Millennial practicing Christians say it is wrong to evangelize (47%).

In fact, they are more likely than non-Christians (20%) and lapsed Christians (17%) to *strongly* agree that "it is wrong to share one's personal beliefs with someone of a different faith in hopes that they will one day share the same faith" (28%).

At the same time, two out of three Millennials believe being a witness about Jesus is part of their faith (65%)

and strongly agree that "the best thing that could ever happen to someone is for them to come to know Jesus" (68%)—a strong majority, but a smaller proportion than among older adults (82%).

Almost two in five practicing Christians say they have no non-Christian friends or family members (38%).

This is true of only one in five Millennials (21%), who are also more likely than older Christians to have seven or more non-Christians friends (32% vs. 25%).

More than half report having two or fewer conversations about faith with a non-Christian during the past year (56%).

Not surprisingly, those with at least seven non-Christian friends or family members are more likely than those with none to have talked about faith 10 or more times (27% vs. 9%)

Those who had at least one conversation about faith came away more confident and eager to talk with others.

Nearly nine out of 10 say they are more confident in their own faith (86%) and seven out of 10 report being more eager to share their faith again (71%).

KEY FINDINGS AMONG NON-CHRISTIANS & LAPSED CHRISTIANS

Seven in 10 say they are not "on a quest for spiritual truth" (71%).

Three-quarters of lapsed Christians (76%) and two-thirds of "nones" (67%) say so. However, about half of non-Christians who belong to another religion think of themselves as on a spiritual quest (46%).

Thirty-eight percent report they "don't have any questions about faith"—but some are more apt than others to say so.

Atheists and agnostics (as one might expect) are least interested in exploring spiritual matters (57%) compared to one in five religious non-Christians (21%) and three in 10 lapsed Christians (30%).

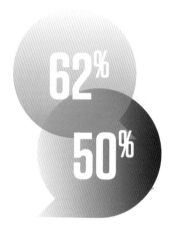

The top qualities they would look for in a person with whom to talk about faith are "listens without judgment" (62%) and "does not force a conclusion" (50%).

However, only a minority would say the Christians they know personally possess these qualities (34% listens without judgment; 26% does not force a conclusion).

Some non-Christians say they might be more interested in Christianity if they had more evidence (44%) and the faith had a better reputation (34%).

Practicing Christians, however, tend to underestimate the importance of evidence (14%) and reputation (23%) to non-Christians' interest

Those who engage in regular conversations about faith are much more open to exploring faith than those who don't.

For example, half who have engaged six or more times on faith in the past year are open to a one-on-one faith conversation, compared to one in six who've had no such encounters (48% vs. 18%).

INTRODUCTION

An early hallmark of Jesus' ministry was delegation. He worked strategically to entrust his message of the coming of God's kingdom to people capable of remembering and faithfully transmitting that message to others—along with express instructions to pass it on. Famously, his parting words to his disciples, known as the Great Commission, are a mandate for worldwide discipleship, a process that requires evangelistic work—*gospel* work.

In the first generations after Jesus gave those instructions, Christianity experienced explosive, exponential growth in spite of profound internal and external challenges. Theological debate, cultural skepticism and government-sponsored persecution complicated the carrying forward of the gospel. But within a few centuries, that good news had been preached from Britain to India, inland Africa to China, resulting in one of the most remarkable stories of global transformation in history. The spread of the gospel changed the course of history—and has in every century since. Although Christian history has been fraught with failures as well as successes of mission, one

Christianity in the United States has always been in a perpetual state of reinvention, but cultural and demographic changes over recent decades have led to a season of unprecedented challenge

thing is certain: The original commission from Jesus has been carried forward, generation to generation, across the centuries.

With that continuing mission have always come challenges, and this generation is faced with plenty of obstacles to effective evangelism. Christianity in the United States has always been in a perpetual state of reinvention, but cultural and demographic changes over recent decades have led to a season of unprecedented challenge. The overall number of practicing Christians is falling, against a cultural backdrop that is increasingly tribal and difficult to define.

Significant societal upheavals have led us here. They include the innovative disruptions of the Internet and social media, generational shifts accompanying the coming of age of Millennials and Generation Z, and increasing political rifts between Christian conservatives and progressives. Complicating this turmoil are factors actively tearing at the social fabric: the breakdown of institutions such as the traditional family; the rapidly diversifying racial and ethnic makeup of America; the revelation of sexual aggression and abuse in once-hallowed religious, artistic, academic and political spheres; and highly public violence such as terrorist attacks and mass murders in community spaces.

What or who can be trusted anymore? It feels to many that threatening waters are rising fast and common ground is in short supply.

Historically, the Christian community has been a source of stability and encouragement in the face of uncertainty and suffering. But today's difficulties are compounded by the fact that practicing Christians are not immune to the destabilization felt so widely. Christians in America are fewer and less unified than at any time in recent memory—and few show signs of knowing what comes next.

This trajectory cannot correct itself. Difficulties for Christians will likely increase in coming years, especially as perceptions of our reliability and reputation suffer. Besides further demographic shifts,

Our calling is not demographic dominance. The Church's mission is to spread the message of saving, sacrificial love and ultimate hope that Jesus commissioned his followers to proclaim.

as the last of the Elders pass and Boomers age out of dominant influence, it's likely that public perception of Christian faith in America will continue to decline, seen by non-Christians as irrelevant, politically corrupt or morally hypocritical. Many in Gen Z, whose oldest members are on the cusp of their 20s, feel little cultural pressure to maintain a faith identity, Christian or otherwise.

If you feel these combined dynamics point to an existential crisis for the Church, you're not wrong. But the crisis may not be the one that comes immediately to mind.

Ask the Right Question

Our calling as Christians is not demographic dominance. It's not even about cultural survival, or about securing the faith of the next generation (as important as that is). The Church's mission is to spread the message of saving, sacrificial love and ultimate hope that Jesus commissioned his followers to proclaim. It's not about numeric growth; that's just a byproduct. It's about the good news.

Losing cultural ground? We can cope with that.

Losing the gospel? That's a different story.

Are we faithfully sharing the good news? The answer to *that*—not a mere count of conversions— is a true indication of the Church's flourishing. Cultural decline and fragmentation cannot threaten the existence or integrity of the Church as a gospel community, but the failure to share our faith certainly can. We must ask ourselves how we are faring in our role as heirs of Jesus' call to the apostles.

What Is a Lapsed Christian?

· · · · · · · · · · · · · · · · · ·

Lapsed Christians are the largest group self-identified Christians in the US; they make up more than two-thirds of those who identify as Christian. They may hold some measure of Christian belief, but they do not prioritize faith either internally (by considering it personally important) or externally (by regular involvement in a local church).

One factor at work may be that most lapsed Christians' family of origin did not highly value faith in their childhood home, especially compared with practicing Christians' families.

"Faith was very important to my family's identity when I was a child." *(% strongly agree)*

Lapsed Christians 23%
Practicing Christians 70%

On this count, Barna's recent research, commissioned by Alpha USA, suggests reason for concern. The study was designed to assess both active Christians' and non-Christians' perceptions and experiences related to faith-sharing and spiritual seeking.* Researchers interviewed two groups of people: *practicing Christians* (in Barna's definition, those who say their faith is very important in their life and have attended church within the past month) and all other US adults (which includes both non-Christians and people who identify as Christian but don't prioritize or practice the faith, who we call "lapsed Christians").

From the findings emerge three key realities:

1. **Evangelism Erosion:** The forces of cultural and religious change are eroding the landscape of evangelism.
2. **Blurred Maps:** Christians' perceptions of the landscape *and of themselves* are often hazy or wide of the mark.
3. **Fertile Soil:** Real opportunities remain for evangelism, but effective faith-sharing today looks different from the past.

As we will see, Christians do not have a united front in support of evangelism. Additionally, many lag behind their non-Christian peers in the kinds of diverse relationships that are desirable for cultivating a healthy evangelistic culture and opportunities to share Christ. What's more, their relational and conversational skills are sometimes lacking.

Failure to proclaim the gospel demands that Christians ask hard questions of ourselves before turning our eyes outward. It would be easy to assign responsibility for declining numbers to cultural factors. But the easy explanation doesn't fit the data. We who are entrusted with the message of Jesus are ultimately responsible for faithfully communicating it. What is it about our community or our presentation that is disconnected from the needs of our neighbors? We must do our best to ensure they can hear the good news shared with them in a way

What has gone so wrong with our gospel presentation that a majority of Christians hesitate to wholeheartedly support it?

For a complete methodology of this project, see pp. 105.

both faithful to the call of Jesus and framed for cultural intelligibility, so that they can give the message of hope and life a fair hearing.

This begins with us. Some of the most troubling numbers emerging from the data are not about "them" at all. A majority of practicing Christians does not consistently support evangelism, and 47 percent of Millennial Christians believe it is flat-out wrong to evangelize. This invites us to ask difficult questions, including what has gone so wrong with our gospel presentation that a majority of Christians hesitates to wholeheartedly support it.

Compounding this are factors that depress Christians' ability to reach out to others skillfully—most conspicuously, that Christians are the faith group least likely to have friends who are different from them.

Additionally, Christian perceptions of what motivates non-Christians to consider or move toward faith are different from the actual felt experiences of non-Christians. The low level of spiritual hunger reported by most non-Christians is one example, along with their desire for more compelling evidence for the faith and negative impressions of Christianity's reputation. Overall, Christians perceive non-Christians to be considerably more interested in spiritual things in general, and Christianity in particular, than they actually are.

Christians must realize we are not doing evangelism on a clean slate. Cultural perceptions and Christianity's poor reputation are actively de-converting people raised in church and hardening non-Christians against evangelistic efforts.

Understand Ourselves & Others

In order to be engaged and effective in our call to share the good news, we must understand and respond to these changing realities. But in perhaps the most eye-opening results from Barna's research, Christians are often poorly equipped in the relational skills needed to navigate a new era of sharing the gospel. Their self-understanding, and their perceptions of non-Christians, vary widely from the perspectives of those outside the faith. Additionally, the overall relational capital and skill set of Christians are often inadequate to maintain a trusted place in public dialog and to earn a fair hearing from those who might consider faith in Jesus Christ.

There is a unique opportunity for the US Church to return to its core identity during this time of transition. Against the backdrop of changing generations we see signs for optimism. While faith in America will never look the same as for our grandparents, it can be strong, authentic and resilient for whatever the future has in store. After all, you don't pass the same message along for 20 centuries unless there's something in it that can transcend cultural shifts.

Above all, we ought to keep hold of hope. History has seen the Church flourish time and again in discouraging evangelistic environments. Today is a wake-up call that can inspire us to grow, to reconnect with the call to be and make disciples, and to press forward into deeper and more radically countercultural faith. Rather than discouragement, this research can profoundly encourage us—if we are willing to embrace it realistically and respond humbly.

Seen rightly, our unprecedented challenges can become untapped opportunities. But only if we begin to understand them. ✳

Today is a wake-up call that can inspire us to reconnect with the call to be and make disciples

1 EVANGELISM EROSION

The proportion of Christians in America is declining, a clear trend that is likely to continue—especially because Gen Z (who are not reflected in this study as a separate group) self-identifies as atheist at twice the rate of US adults overall (13% vs. 7%).[1] Barna tracking data since 1996 shows a sharp rise in those identifying as atheist, agnostic or "none" / no faith, alongside a nearly matching decline in "born again" Christians.

Forecasting in detail the impact of coming generations—who are all culturally "post-Christendom" and mostly "post-Christian" in their worldview—is impossible. But it's safe to say the assumption that most people have been raised with similar faith practices or even a common religious language is already outdated.

What's at stake if Christian evangelism is changing? Perhaps more than first meets the eye. Besides the obvious—that a decline in new believers will contribute to an overall decline in Christianity—there will likely be wider social effects.

To get a glimpse of the shape those effects may take, Christians' evangelistic habits can act as a canary in the social coal mine. In examining how Christians share faith, we also gain insight into the strength of our social fabric, our cultural habits surrounding religious

(Continued on p. 24.)

If evangelism is eroding, we must examine its wider context to understand and respond

KNOW YOUR AUDIENCE

In approaching evangelism with those outside the Christian church, audience matters. Lapsed Christians, religious non-Christians and atheists / agnostics / nones express varying degrees of spiritual interest—and name very different obstacles keeping them from being more interested in learning about Christianity. These opinions offer clues for how to approach faith conversations, depending on who you are talking to.

● Lapsed Christians ○ Religious non-Christians ● Atheists / agnostics / nones

I consider myself to be a spiritual person

62% 81%
48%

I have unanswered spiritual questions

40% 56%
36%

I experience a general sense of emptiness

29% 46%
33%

I am curious about who God is

52% 54%
33%

I am interested in exploring faiths that are different from my own

32% 54%
40%

I am seeking something spiritually better

30% 56%
30%

I'D BE MORE INTERESTED IN LEARNING ABOUT CHRISTIANITY IF...

Lapsed Christians

With more experience in the church, lapsed Christians may have more baggage—expressed in a desire to see Christians acting differently. They also seem to have missed out on having a personal spiritual experience—something that possibly led them to leaving the church or the faith in the first place.

Most important

 31% I saw various churches in my community working together more

 32% I had an eye-opening spiritual experience myself

 31% The Christians I knew were more humble and aware of their shortcomings

Least important

 13% The Christians I know were more articulate about their faith

Religious Non-Christians

As part of other religious traditions, this group is already willing to believe in the supernatural, but they see Christianity as lacking in evidence. They also point toward the church's reputation and its ability to work with others.

Most important

 31% Christianity had better evidence to support it

 31% Christianity had a better reputation

 29% I saw various churches in my community working together more

Least important

 10% The Christians I know demonstrated a more vibrant personal faith

Atheists / Agnostics / Nones

Unsurprisingly, this group is most concerned with evidence. Relatedly, they might believe if they could personally experience it for themselves. And, once again, the reputation of Christianity gets in their way.

Most important

 44% Christianity had better evidence to support it

 35% Christianity had a better reputation

 29% I had an eye-opening spiritual experience myself

Least important

 10% The Christians I know were more articulate about their faith

n=1,001 US adults who are not practicing Christians; May 2018.

From Cross to CrossFit?

· · · · · · · · · · · · · · · · · · ·

A recent Harvard study researched the similarities between churches and a number of non-religious organizations, including CrossFit gyms. "Religion is changing," said Casper ter Kuile, author of the study *How We Gather*. He and his coauthor, Angie Thurston, traced a series of 10 organizations from an initial pool of 100, and rated them according to six qualities historically associated with faith gatherings: community, personal transformation, social transformation, purpose-finding, creativity and accountability.[2]

Their research reveals that some people, Millennials especially, are looking to CrossFit and similar groups to play the role traditionally reserved for religious community. They expect this trend to grow as more people shift to life away from church but recognize their need for the input and outlet of a local community.

dialog and our receding abilities to maintain diverse relationships. As we will see, Christian faith-sharing relates to all of these. If evangelism—a social action that depends on unlike people considering the merits of shared belief and practice—is eroding, we must examine its wider context to understand and respond.

"Erosion" is an apt metaphor for the changes affecting evangelism in America. Rather than sharp breaks or explosive damage, waves of changes—some large, some small—are gradually wearing away faith-sharing habits, values and skills.

Three trends emerging from the data demonstrate this erosion:

- *America is "de-churching" and increasingly isolated.*
- *Most people do not feel a "God-shaped hole."*
- *Cultural fragmentation complicates evangelism.*

Let's examine each one.

People Are De-Churching & Getting Lonelier

Along with declining Christian identity, churchgoing is in decline. In 2003, three-quarters of US self-identified Christians reported attending church at least once in the previous six months (77%). Today, just 60 percent of Christians say they attended a worship service during the past six months. So even among the diminishing number of US adults who check the "Christian" box, church involvement is becoming less common.

How Often US Adults Attend Religious Services

% among US adults 18 and older

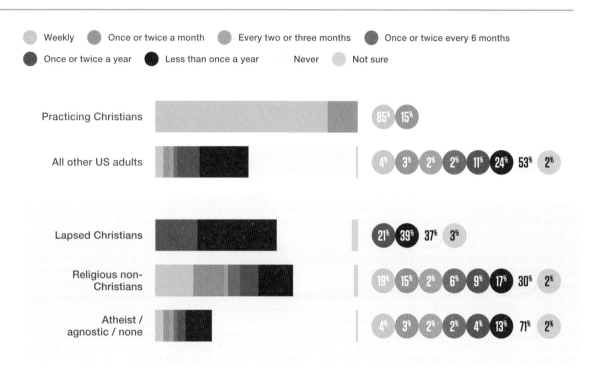

n=1,992 US adults 18 and older; May 2018.

Besides the accompanying shift in spiritual alignment, church involvement is not being replaced in terms of social capital. Most Elders were raised in a world where it was assumed one attended a house of worship, where one found a network of believers who offered social support, friendship and many other benefits. As church involvement has dropped off, however, few alternatives have arisen to take its place. Only about one-quarter of US adults who are not practicing Christians report belonging to a spiritual community (23%). The communal aspect of church is simply not being replaced—at least not with relationships that are overtly spiritual (see "From Cross to CrossFit?" on p. 24).

SHARING FAITH FORMS FAITH
Q&A with Michelle Jones

Michelle D. Jones is a pastor and writer serving at Imago Dei Community Church in Portland, Oregon, and a sought-after conference speaker, workshop facilitator and preacher who serves diverse audiences in the US and abroad. She is also an award-winning sitcom writer and producer. Her credits include In The House, Parent 'Hood *and* In Living Color, *for which she earned an Emmy nomination and an NAACP Image Award. Michelle has a passion for women, singles, creative communities, mentorship and sound gospel teaching. Read more of her work at LifeElastic.wordpress.com*

Q *What do you see as the natural links between evangelism and spiritual formation?*

A "I catch 'em, you clean 'em." That's what a leader in a well-known evangelism ministry said to me when I told him my area of ministry is spiritual formation. We had a good laugh, but the truth is, Christians do typically view formation as *following* a faith decision versus interacting with it. But I think the relationship between growth and the gospel is more complex and beautiful, developing and deepening over time. The unfortunate consequence of the common view is that it deprioritizes evangelism for people who are already "caught." That leaves them ill-prepared to share their good news with others.

In the past, I focused my attention more on personal growth than on evangelism. I see now that what I and others have unwittingly done is equip an army to feed and care for itself while leaving it unprepared for a wider war. Sharing faith has to be taught as an integral part of formation.

So much of what I do on a daily basis involves helping an individual grow after he or she becomes a Christ-follower. I don't think the average staff pastor like me spends enough time teaching how evangelism can be *formative*, not just proof of formation. Moreover, we replicate leaders who instruct and shepherd people, but rarely train them how to share their faith should the opportunity present itself. We talk about "salt and light," but those images of faith (meant to benefit culture) too often get lost in our consumer-shaped ministries.

As believers we are stewards of our gifts and calling, but we also steward the attention of others. We give those who encounter us a glimpse—for better or worse—of Christ on earth. When we give ourselves to evangelism, we are lifting him up and presenting him to a world crying out for a Savior, instead of just secreting him away as a tool for our own personal sanctification.

Q ***In your experience in a very secular city, what kinds of evidence do non-Christian friends and neighbors find compelling?***

A While Portland is a "secular city," it is also, like many other places, a *searching* city—and one that wears its probing on its sleeve. I

"

The relationship between growth and the gospel is complex and beautiful, developing and deepening over time

mention that because a label like "secular" can imply a lack of desire for the mysterious, the spiritual or the religious, and that's not the case. For many searching places, the greatest weakness is also the greatest strength: It is open to pretty much anything.

But in such a place, "evidence" does not automatically mean "proof" or something visible to draw a person to the sensibleness of a belief. In my experience, the concept of God / Christ / Spirit as *Creator* is one of the most compelling ways to engage friends and neighbors, to draw their attention to faith. An understanding of how creation cares for us as we care for it shows the value of humanity to a "Supreme Being." *This is evidence*. The order and beauty of human form, creativity and the wider glory of nature speaks to a culture floundering in uncertainty.

The gospel, like Apple products (to use the words of Steve Jobs), is "elegantly designed, and useable right out of the box." When we locate and communicate the simple and profound beauty of divine wisdom present in nature and art, it speaks and is understood. It's convincing evidence.

When we offer this evidence, it's important to remember that *evangelism* is how we love the world, as God does, but *conversion* is the work of the Holy Spirit. Live the truth you tell. Tell the truth you live. The rest is God's business. When we wed ourselves to the idea that we are responsible for making people believe, we put ourselves in the place of the Savior or the Spirit. We take glory that doesn't belong to us.

An agenda-driven, score-keeping Christian is the easiest thing to sniff out. Most of our seeming inauthenticity comes from the impression that we are keeping score—waiting to notch our belt if someone accepts Christ. Or we give off the impression that the person we're "presenting evidence" to is not as acceptable to us as they would be if they came to faith. That can make people feel like we are insincere or untrustworthy. And they would be correct.

Listening is an act of love. Sharing faith is a gift offered from a place of humility and generosity.

Q *What element of sharing faith do Christians need to rediscover today?*

A Listening as an act of love. Sharing faith is not a one-size-fits-all proposition. It's not an information dump or a game of show-and-tell. It is an answer to an inquiry, an invitation to the lost and a gift offered from a place of humility and generosity.

Everything Jesus did was personal before it was anything else. He listened to what people said to him and extracted from it the cry of their hearts, their suspect motives or their uncertainties. God knows everything, yet he "inclines his ear" to us—not for his sake, but for ours. There is something kind and big-hearted in that act.

Listening makes room for people. In a culture that places high value on acceptance, this is no small thing. When we make space first for who people are, and then for what matters to them, only then can we know how to offer ourselves and our faith to them.

Listening is the first duty of a servant. Without it, he or she has no way of knowing what the "master" requires. When we share our faith, we are servants, not sages. We are the poor, holding out only what we have received by the grace of Another. And when we listen, we are giving ourselves to others—in that moment saying, "Master, what do you require?"

We are spiritually formed by and in the love of God in Christ. Evangelism is the fruit and the root of our formation. To give the grace we have been given is not only evidence of our transformation; it is itself transforming. Every opportunity to share our faith with others challenges us to live out what we say we believe. And every time we refuse to shrink away from that responsibility, we are strengthened in our faith and as a witness. ✳

"I belong to a spiritual community where I can explore questions of meaning or faith."

% among US non-Christians and lapsed Christians 18 and older

- Agree strongly
- Agree somewhat
- Disagree somewhat
- Disagree strongly

6%
17%
48%
29%

n=1,001 US adults who are not practicing Christians, May 2018.

The number of people who tell Barna they feel lonely or isolated has increased in the past decade from 10 to 20 percent. The increase in loneliness reported by Americans is likely due at least in part to their disengagement from communities of faith. The void has been only partially filled by the rise of virtual networks. People online can learn about faith, dialog with others, give to causes they believe in and even experience some measure of shared worship. But while real connection can and does occur in such digital spaces, the community aspects of a local church are not sufficiently replicated online.

For example, in new research among 18- to 29-year-olds with a Christian background, Barna found that young adults who are most committed to practicing their faith today also tend to be more relationally well-rounded. Eight out of 10 report having a close, intimate friend (83%) and three-quarters say they have someone, other than a family member, to whom they can turn for advice (77%). On the other hand, ex-Christians or "prodigals" (as they are called in that study), are less likely to have a close friend (53%) or to have someone they can turn to for advice (49%).[3]

The de-churching of America is not the *only* factor making people lonelier than ever—but it's certainly *a* factor.

The "God-shaped hole" is simply not a conscious part of most non-Christians' experience

Spiritual Hunger Is Limited . . . or Called by Another Name

There are stark contrasts between practicing Christians and other adults' perceptions related to their spirituality. For instance, when asked if they consider themselves to be "on a quest for spiritual truth," three-quarters of practicing Christians say yes (76%). In contrast, roughly equal proportions of lapsed Christians (77%) and the religiously unaffiliated (sometimes called "nones," 72%) say they are *not*. Meanwhile, about half of non-Christians who belong to another religion think of themselves as on a spiritual quest (46%).

Questions in a similar vein further highlight differences between Christian and non-Christian perceptions related to spirituality. Only one in nine adults who aren't practicing Christians strongly agrees that "my religious faith is very important in my life today" (11%). Only seven percent *strongly* agree they are seeking something spiritually better (25% *somewhat* vs. 30% somewhat and 35% strongly agree among practicing Christians). When asked if they agree with the statement "I am seeking something spiritually better," Buddhist, Hindu and Muslim respondents tend to agree (56%); atheists, agnostics and nones, on the other hand, disagree (70%). Similarly, when asked if they feel "a general sense of emptiness," two-thirds of the religiously unaffiliated disagree (67%).

A sense of spiritual need—sometimes called the "God-shaped hole"—is simply not a conscious part of most non-Christians' experience.

Several other findings serve to reinforce this

How Do People Practice Spirituality?

. . . .

When asked to describe activities they consider part of practicing their faith or spirituality, non-Christians give a range of responses. Here is a sampling of their answers:

- Cycling
- Fishing
- Gardening
- Sex
- Marijuana
- Volleyball
- Prayer
- Being kind and decent
- Being good and charitable
- Bible reading
- Bird watching
- Charity
- Walking outdoors
- Reading and discussing spiritual books
- Hospice volunteering

picture of overall spiritual indifference. Atheists and agnostics (as one might expect) are *least* interested in exploring spiritual matters; six in 10 report they "don't have any questions about faith" (58%), compared to just one in five religious non-Christians (19%).

Two-thirds of all US adults who do not practice Christianity say spirituality plays little or no role in their everyday lives.

How US Adults (Who Are Not Practicing Christians) Prioritize Spirituality

% among US non-Christians and lapsed Christians 18 and older

- Spirituality is the most important thing in my life
- Spirituality is as important as anything else in my life
- Spirituality plays a minor role in my life
- Spirituality plays no role in my life

6%	26%	41%	27%

n=1,001 US adults 18 and older who are not practicing Christians; May 2018.

Men are more likely to say there's no role for spirituality in their lives (33% vs. 22% women), and women more likely to rank it as important (36% vs. 27% men).

Similar to how they rate the role of spirituality in their lives, most Americans do not report having high levels of "unanswered spiritual questions." Buddhists, Hindus and Muslims are more likely than other non-Christians to agree they have such questions (55%), and to agree that "something feels missing from my life" (53%).

Barna analysts suspect a cultural trend of *secularizing the sacred* is partly to blame for overall spiritual apathy. Longings and practices that have historically been spiritual are increasingly discussed in terms

Spiritual Mindsets of US Adults

% strongly + somewhat agree among US adults 18 and older

Dark = Strongly agree, Light = Somewhat agree

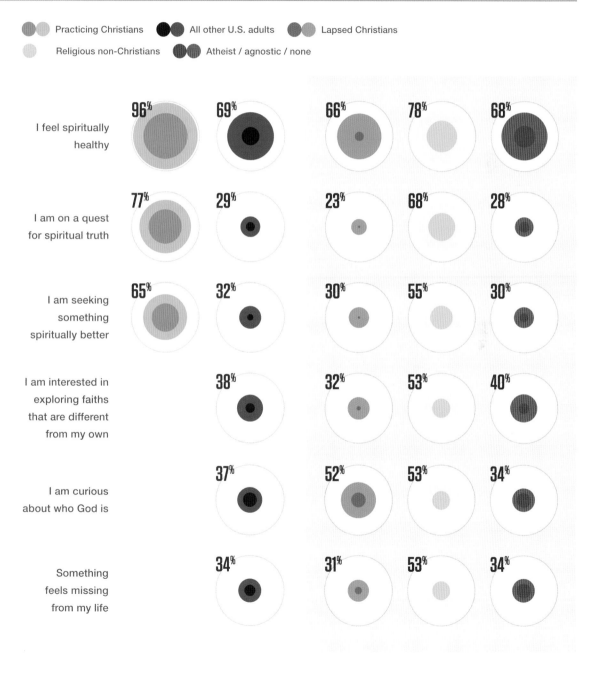

Practicing Christians   All other U.S. adults   Lapsed Christians

Religious non-Christians   Atheist / agnostic / none

	Practicing Christians	All other U.S. adults	Lapsed Christians	Religious non-Christians	Atheist / agnostic / none
I feel spiritually healthy	96%	69%	66%	78%	68%
I am on a quest for spiritual truth	77%	29%	23%	68%	28%
I am seeking something spiritually better	65%	32%	30%	55%	30%
I am interested in exploring faiths that are different from my own		38%	32%	53%	40%
I am curious about who God is		37%	52%	53%	34%
Something feels missing from my life		34%	31%	53%	34%

that are *not* spiritual. For many people, for example, "meditation" has become "mindfulness"—placing what was once a spiritual practice into the category of mental awareness. To borrow a consumer term, a church is no longer the only storefront on the block selling purpose, relational connection and a sense of belonging. Instead, human impulses to connect and give are diverted into new channels. Money once given to tithe or a deacon's fund might now be donated to a secular nonprofit or GoFundMe for a sick friend. Social functions once promoted in church bulletins are organized on social media, include a wide invite list and gather in decentralized locations rather than the congregation's "fellowship hall" of 30 years ago. What was once searching for God is now "looking for meaning and purpose." Simplicity and a desire to make a difference are divested of spiritual connection and re-envisioned as ways to benefit self and promote general wellbeing.

One example of the trend is Adriene Mishler, host of the YouTube channel Yoga with Adriene, which currently boasts more than 4 million subscribers. Her brand of yoga as exercise and "grounding practice" is nearly devoid of the spiritual roots of the tradition. Yogis of the past were teachers of spiritual wisdom before anything else, but Yoga with Adriene features videos like "Yoga for Weight Loss," "Yoga for Creativity" and "Yoga for Text Neck." It is a thoroughly secular space. "Find what feels good" is the mantra her followers "recite with almost evangelical fervor," observes *The Guardian*.[4]

The availability of secular outlets for spiritual impulses is not harmful in itself, but it is symptomatic of a culture losing a shared language of spirituality—and even losing agreement that spirituality is meaningful at all.

Thus, faith-sharing today should most often start with an assumption that most people do not deeply feel their spiritual need, at least not in a way they recognize or describe in those terms.

Activities People Consider a Part of Their Spirituality

% among US non-Christians and lapsed Christians 18 and older

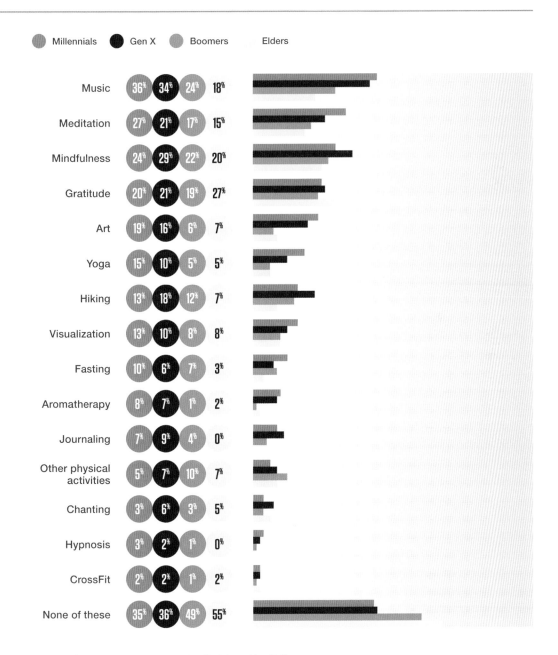

Millennials   Gen X   Boomers   Elders

	Millennials	Gen X	Boomers	Elders
Music	36%	34%	24%	18%
Meditation	27%	21%	17%	15%
Mindfulness	24%	29%	22%	20%
Gratitude	20%	21%	19%	27%
Art	19%	16%	6%	7%
Yoga	15%	10%	5%	5%
Hiking	13%	18%	12%	7%
Visualization	13%	10%	8%	8%
Fasting	10%	6%	7%	3%
Aromatherapy	8%	7%	1%	2%
Journaling	7%	9%	4%	0%
Other physical activities	5%	7%	10%	7%
Chanting	3%	6%	3%	5%
Hypnosis	3%	2%	1%	0%
CrossFit	2%	2%	1%	2%
None of these	35%	36%	49%	55%

n=1,001 US adults who are not practicing Christians, May 2018.

Evangelism Is More Complex

Previous generations saw enormous success with relatively monolithic evangelism strategies such as mass campaigns, widespread adoption of "lifestyle evangelism" and small "seeker-sensitive" evangelistic Bible studies. While these approaches may still be effective in some contexts, the world today is different from decades past and "results may vary." Between the de-churching of America and the decline of spiritual hunger, there is no longer a single recipe for what predictably compels non-Christians to give the gospel their true consideration (but there are necessary ingredients, as we will see in a later chapter).

Perhaps an analogy, though a bit morbid, could be drawn with the history of warfare. In previous generations, large-scale battles with vast masses of general-duty troops were the norm. But warfare has gradually shifted and is now characterized by small conflicts often led by highly trained or specialized units responding to a particular kind of opponent.

While evangelism is obviously not combat (and Christians are, by and large, wisely moving away from the militant language popular in earlier eras of evangelism), thoughtlessly adopting used-to-be-effective tactics is similar to leading a cavalry charge against modern tanks. It will probably not be effective, and it may even cause more harm than good.

Along with effective strategies, what Christians believe about evangelism is also changing. Between 1993 and 2017, Barna saw dramatic changes in Christians' positions on sharing their faith. Just one in 10 Christians in 1993 who had a conversation about faith believed evangelism was the job of the local church (10%). Twenty-five years later, three in 10 said so (29%). Nine out of 10 agreed in 1993 that "every Christian has a responsibility to share their faith" (89%). Only two-thirds said so in 2017 (64%).[5]

Perhaps most tellingly, the percentage who say "I would avoid discussions about my faith if my non-Christian friend would reject me" has risen from 33 to 44 percent in the past 25 years.

There is not a single recipe for what compels non-Christians to give the gospel their true consideration

They are not wrong to perceive increased social risks.

In his book *Good Faith,* Barna president David Kinnaman examines shifting cultural currents surrounding people of faith and perceptions of how they practice their convictions. Research for that book found a startling six in 10 Americans believe that any "attempt to convert others" to one's own faith is "extreme." More than eight out of 10 atheists, agnostics and nones say so! To be clear: A majority of US adults, and the vast majority of non-religious adults (83%), believe that evangelism is religiously extreme.[6]

. . . .

Growing social isolation and diminishing spiritual interest do not make a friendly environment for sharing one's faith. How accurately are Christians assessing the cultural situation? As the overall culture of faith-sharing erodes, how are they responding? How well (or poorly) are they adapting? Are they well-poised to share their faith in keeping with the historic mission of Jesus's followers? ✳

Evangelizing Christian Youth

. . . .

Among US adults who do not practice Christianity today, two-thirds were raised in a Christian family (63%).

About half of atheists, agnostics and nones were raised in a Christian family (55%). Nearly all lapsed Christians were raised in a Christian family (97%).

Exposure to vibrant family faith does not always translate to a child's personal belief. Young people raised in Christian communities are in the process of considering Christianity as much as anyone—and their Christian parents, and older sisters and brothers in the faith, should consider how they can invite them to a life of following Jesus.

HOPE FOR AWAKENING
Q&A with Tim Keller

Timothy Keller is the founding pastor of Redeemer Presbyterian Church in Manhattan, and chairman and cofounder of Redeemer City to City (CTC), which helps plant churches in global cities. Dr. Keller has published multiple bestselling Christian books, including The Reason for God.

Q *You've spent a lot of time researching historical revivals. How do gospel movements change a culture?*

A By changing people. The gospel changes lives; it gives people a new identity. But the gospel also creates a community around it. That community doesn't fit into anyone's categories. If the gospel is going to change a whole city or culture, something extraordinary must happen. It's not just addition, it's multiplication—through a community.

The very beginning of the Christian church was this kind of explosive movement, but it's hard to study because it was so long ago. The gospel movements we can examine more closely have happened in the last 300 years. They're often called "awakenings." They're sometimes called revivals. We at City to City like to call them "gospel movements."

The First Great Awakening, for example, happened during much of the 18th century in Britain and America. It was led by people like John and Charles Wesley and George Whitefield, and it was massive. There are people who make good arguments that the reason why England did not have a bloody revolution the way the French did at the end of the 1700s was because of the social healing that resulted from that long-term revival.

More recently—about 1907—there was a revival at a big Bible conference in Pyongyang, which is now in North Korea. Over the next 70 years or so the Korean church grew from zero to something like 20 or 30 percent of the population.

Something similar happened in the East African Revival, between the late 1920s into the 1950s. What happened in those decades is the reason that today there are at least 9 million Anglicans in Uganda. For comparison, there are about 2 million Episcopalians in America. This was an exponential movement.

Q *How do gospel movements happen?*

A There is a spectrum of opinion. At one end, we're told there's nothing we can do. We just hope God will do it when he's going to do it. At the other end of the spectrum people say, "Absolutely you can make this happen. Go out. Organize. You can have a revival if you try hard enough, know the technique, and scale it up."

The truth is in the middle. A spiritual awakening is clearly a supernatural phenomenon. But we have a responsibility to work for it.

A spiritual awakening is clearly a supernatural phenomenon. But we have a responsibility to work for it.

David Martyn Lloyd-Jones, a great British preacher who studied and experienced these movements, came up with the perfect illustration: Elijah laying out the wood, and God sending the fire. That's how these awakenings come. We can't ignite the fire. But we can lay the wood out.

The wood is the three essential elements needed for real revival.

First, *gospel rediscovery*. This requires finding a balanced gospel again: the truth that we are saved by faith alone, but not by faith that remains alone. We're saved by the grace of Christ, but that changes our hearts so we want to obey him. We want God. Dr. Lloyd-Jones pictures it like managing to balance on the peak of a mountain without slipping down either face of it into heresy. Both fundamentalism and liberalism pull us down the mountain, just in opposite directions. Both lose the power of the gospel by slipping into either legalism or relativism. A lot of very conservative churches need to rediscover grace, a lot of more liberal churches need to rediscover the cross. We need a large-scale rediscovery of the beauty of a balanced gospel. We must get back to the mountaintop.

Secondly, *contextual creativity*. The gospel never changes, but because culture and history do, the way we communicate it changes. For example, the First Great Awakening with Wesley and Whitefield basically happened by means of preaching in the open air—streets and fields. That was radical. For centuries in Europe, the message was solely preached on Sunday from the local pulpit. People were expected to come to the preacher. But in the 18th century, after the Industrial Revolution, people were leaving the countryside and cramming into cities. They were disembedded from their extended families, and they just weren't showing up in church. It was radical, but John Wesley and company originated a new way of preaching that went into open public spaces. They were creative.

Finally, *extraordinary prayer*. What do I mean by extraordinary? It means letting our prayer for the gospel to move exceed ordinary means: quiet time, daily devotions, prayer in church. Do that. But also notice that one consistent thing in the histories of these great gospel movements is prayer that is somehow outside the box, unusual, different. One famous example is a room in Herrnhut—in Saxony, Germany—in the home of the Moravian Count Nicolaus von Zinzendorf. His community began a prayer meeting for worldwide evangelization and committed to having someone pray in that room 24 hours a day. And they did. *For a hundred years*. Today we remember it as the 100-Year Prayer Meeting. That's extraordinary prayer.

These three elements are key to preparing for the "fire." When it ignites, we see wide signs of a gospel-renewed city or region. There are visible outcomes when people find faith en masse. Generosity is one. Studies show that what we might call evangelical Christians give away a far higher percentage of their income than other people. If 20 or 30 percent of your city become gospel-changed people, the fact of the matter is there would be an explosion of philanthropy.

Also, the gospel creates a certain humility that promotes honest dialog and confession. Today, left-wing and right-wing people hate each other. They are not even civil about their differences anymore. Christians ought to be humbled by the gospel, if they have really heard what the gospel says. They should show respect to people who differ from them, but also be confident and willing to embrace difficult conversations.

Real Christians are humble, bold agents of civility. They act as salt and light, bringing together people who can't even talk to each other because of their hatred. Christians lead the way in confession, forgiveness, reconciliation and listening. If we want revival, we should be agents for the kind of civil society we don't have right now in America.

The faith that comes in these movements changes culture widely as Christians live out their vocations. In the media, we need to show

"

If we want revival, we should be agents for the kind of civil society we don't have right now in America

that there is such a thing as truth. In the art world, we must show that there's such a thing as hope. In technology, we must ask "Should we?" and not just "Can we?" To bring God into all these areas with grace-changed people in the big cities would change society. It would change history.

We *can* work to multiply ordinary gospel ministry, putting ourselves in a place where God could do something history-changing. It reminds me of the moment in *The Chronicles of Narnia* when Aslan tells the children that they will never get back into Narnia the same way twice. We never seem to have a revival the same way twice. We can't, say, study the Welsh Revival of 1904 and try to replicate what worked.

Nobody can force a major revival to happen. Yet I've seen over the years that when people seek revival, seek gospel movements, God often honors that. He responds to our prayer and preparation.

And that desire is part of it. Do we desire this kind of movement enough to dedicate our lives to it? Do we want to see God's spiritual fire come down on our cities and our churches? Do we want to see the gospel run like lightning through the streets? To see lives changed? To see cities changed?

The Psalms talk about a time of the ultimate gospel movement, when every tear will be wiped away, all sin and evil will be destroyed. All smaller gospel movements look forward to that movement. That's the ultimate dawning, the ultimate spring day. And that is our desire today. We seek gospel movements as forerunners to that ultimate hope. ✳

2 BLURRED MAPS

While there remain significant gospel-sharing opportunities—which we will explore in chapter 3—Christians need to begin thinking about evangelism with a posture of introspection. The research shows a dissonance between Christians' perceptions of effective evangelism and the experience of those who do not practice Christianity. Further, there seem to be gaps in key Christian relational skills and habits that are necessary for evangelism.

The distance between Christians' perceptions of themselves and the reality of how they are perceived by others, is nothing short of a wake-up call. There are significant gaps between how Christians perceive their gospel effectiveness and what actually motivates non-Christians to consider faith in Christ. All told, the emerging picture is one of disconnection—though with points to encourage real hope.

The first step for Christians interested in strategic effectiveness in evangelism is getting an accurate lay of the land, even if doing so is uncomfortable. If faith-sharing habits are based solely on Christians' misperceptions, their effectiveness will be diminished—with significant time and resources spent in unhelpful directions. With this in mind, let's outline key areas where Christians need to sharpen their understanding of self and culture and bring into focus the motivations and attitudes of non-Christians who may be open to considering faith.

. . . .

LET'S ASK THE EVANGELIZED ABOUT EVANGELISM

What they say about evangelistic encounters

Lapsed Christians and non-Christians have experienced many different approaches to Christian evangelism. Barna asked people who have had first-hand experience with each of the methods below to tell researchers whether they came away from the encounter *encouraged* or *discouraged* to explore Christianity further.

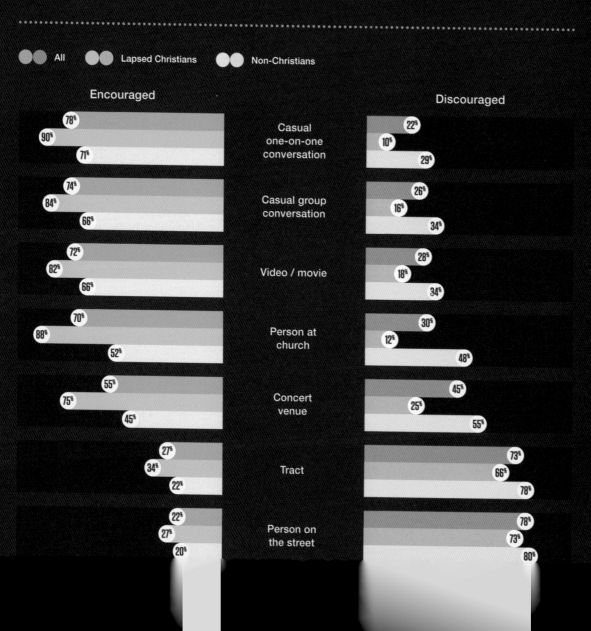

●● All ●● Lapsed Christians ●● Non-Christians

	Encouraged		Discouraged	
Casual one-on-one conversation	All	78%	22%	
	Lapsed Christians	90%	10%	
	Non-Christians	71%	29%	
Casual group conversation	All	74%	26%	
	Lapsed Christians	84%	16%	
	Non-Christians	66%	34%	
Video / movie	All	72%	28%	
	Lapsed Christians	82%	18%	
	Non-Christians	66%	34%	
Person at church	All	70%	30%	
	Lapsed Christians	88%	12%	
	Non-Christians	52%	48%	
Concert venue	All	55%	45%	
	Lapsed Christians	75%	25%	
	Non-Christians	45%	55%	
Tract	All	27%	73%	
	Lapsed Christians	34%	66%	
	Non-Christians	22%	78%	
Person on the street	All	22%	78%	
	Lapsed Christians	27%	73%	
	Non-Christians	20%	80%	

What they say about Christians and conversations

Nearly all non-Christians and lapsed Christians have a friend or family member who practices and prioritizes Christianity—but these believers are not always ideal conversation partners when it comes to faith. Here are the qualities people say they value in a person with whom they would talk about spiritual matters, alongside descriptions they would apply to their Christian friends and family.

● Someone I would talk to about faith   ○ Christians I know personally

	Someone I would talk to about faith	Christians I know personally
Listens without judgment	62%	34%
Does not force a conclusion	50%	26%
Allows others to draw their own conclusions	43%	22%
Confident in sharing their own perspective	33%	28%
Demonstrates interest in other people's story or life	29%	17%
Good at asking questions	27%	16%
Focused on the details of questions	20%	10%
Aware of the inconsistencies in their own perspective	20%	9%
Knows the story of the person they are sharing their faith with	18%	20%
Exhibits a vibrant faith of their own	15%	25%
Good at debating topics	15%	10%
Focused on the emotions behind questions	13%	8%

n=1,001 US adults 18 and older who are not practicing Christians; May 2018

Christians Feel Ready . . . but Not All Are Willing

Only one in 10 practicing Christians feels they don't know how to respond when someone raises a question about faith (10%). Two-thirds feel "gifted" in sharing their faith with others (63%). As these data indicate, most Christians feel at least somewhat equipped to engage in evangelism.

But, to state the obvious, evangelism has no future if followers of Jesus are not *willing* to share their faith with others. No matter what external factors influence non-Christian attitudes toward Christianity, practicing Christians must believe their faith is worth sharing.

And so researchers were surprised to find that, while more than nine out of 10 practicing Christians agree that part of their faith means being a witness for Jesus (96%), and eight out of 10 strongly agree that "the best thing that could ever happen to someone is for them to come to know Jesus" (79%), one-quarter *also* believes it is "wrong to share one's personal beliefs with someone of a different faith in hopes that they will one day share the same faith" (27%). Among Millennials, the percentage is nearly half (47%).

There is a clear generational trend here. But older generations ought to pause before assigning blame to Millennials who are hesitant to evangelize. Younger believers are working to adapt and integrate their faith with a rapidly changing culture. What's needed is cross-generational conversation around an issue that concerns all Christians: the stewardship of Jesus's commission. (See sidebar.)

Generational Differences on Faith-Sharing

% strongly + somewhat agree among US practicing Christians

Dark = Strongly agree
Light = Somewhat agree

Millennials   Gen X   Boomers   Elders

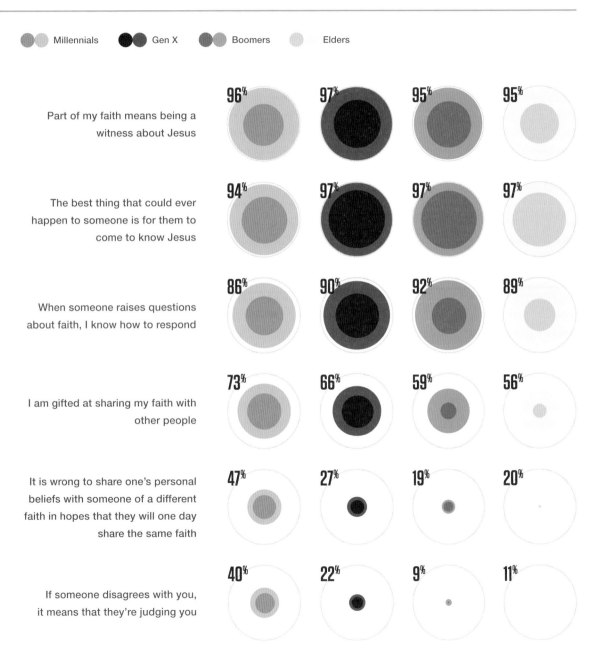

Part of my faith means being a witness about Jesus
96%   97%   95%   95%

The best thing that could ever happen to someone is for them to come to know Jesus
94%   97%   97%   97%

When someone raises questions about faith, I know how to respond
86%   90%   92%   89%

I am gifted at sharing my faith with other people
73%   66%   59%   56%

It is wrong to share one's personal beliefs with someone of a different faith in hopes that they will one day share the same faith
47%   27%   19%   20%

If someone disagrees with you, it means that they're judging you
40%   22%   9%   11%

Some Millennials are unsure about evangelism, or even think of it as morally wrong. (Gen Z teens are not a large enough cohort for separate analysis in this study, but their thoroughly post-Christian posture will likely amplify this stance toward evangelism.) Younger Christians are more *personally* aware of the cultural temperature around spiritual conversations. Among practicing Christians, Millennials report an average (median) of four close friends or family members who practice a faith other than Christianity; most of their Boomer parents and grandparents, by comparison, have just one. Sharing the gospel today is made harder than at any time in recent memory by an overall cultural resistance to conversations that high-light people's differences.

Young Christians' hesitance is understandable. Society today casts a negative light on proselytization that many older Christians do not fully appreciate. As Barna found in research published in *Spiritual Conversations in the Digital Age*, three out of five Christian Millennials believe that people today are more likely than in the past to take offense if they share their faith (65%)—that's far higher than among Boomer Christians (28%).[7] Youth are faced with a very different culture than their parents or grandparents. But as Millennial and Gen Z Christians age into leadership, they will have to answer some important questions.

How hard is too hard to bear witness to what Jesus has done?

How active are they willing to be in service of sharing the gospel?

Will they be willing to find ways to evangelize beyond "living out" their faith?

Leaders who want to equip Christians today to share Jesus with non-believers face an unusual challenge: to first "evangelize" Christians on the importance—and morality—of evangelism.

Christians Feel Ready . . . but Not All Are Able

Once they are willing, some Christians may struggle to make relational connections or gain the conversational skills that effective evangelism requires. Barna found in its comprehensive study among Gen Z that engaged Christian teens are the group *most* likely to say they are comfortable talking about their faith and *least* likely to interact with people who do not share their faith.[8] And in research for Kinnaman's *Good Faith*, the Barna team discovered that evangelicals are less comfortable than other groups in conversation with people they consider significantly different from themselves, such as Muslims or members of the LGBT community.[9]

In the *Reviving Evangelism* study, analysts uncovered significant disparities both between practicing Christians' and others' ideas about the qualities desirable in a faith conversation partner *and* between others' perceptions of the Christians they know compared to those desirable qualities. For example, a majority of practicing Christians believes someone gifted at sharing their faith possesses a number of qualities, including confidence in sharing their own perspective (58%) and an obvious, visible faith of their own (57%). Yet a majority of non-Christians and lapsed Christians values just two qualities in a conversation partner: listening without judgment (62%) and not forcing a conclusion (50%).

Comparing non-Christians' and lapsed Christians' responses to two different questions reveals the second stark disparity: the qualities of "someone I would talk to about faith" versus the qualities of "Christians I know" (see p. 45). Compared to the majority who says they prefer a conversation partner who listens without judgment and a does not force a conclusion, far smaller proportions say those are qualities possessed by Christians they know (34% and 26%, respectively).

These data paint a striking picture of disconnection between Christian ideals of what it means to share faith effectively and the experience of non-Christians—and between non-Christians' perceptions of Christians and Christians' of themselves (see p. 54).

However willing they may be, Christians' *ability* to witness for Christ may be impeded by the simple fact that they don't have meaningful relational connections with non-Christians, or the conversational skills necessary to talk meaningfully about faith.

Most non-Christians value just two qualities in a Christian conversation partner: listening without judgment and not forcing a conclusion

GOOD NEWS FOR NEW GENERATIONS
Q&A with Josh Chen

Josh Chen serves as a missions director for Cru because he is passionate about helping young people experience the goodness of the gospel. He leads a team in Portland, Oregon, with his wife, Wendy.

Q *In your work with Millennials and Gen Z teens, what have you observed about how they think about sharing faith?*

A Each generation must discover the gospel afresh for itself. What sounded like good news to previous generations often sounds like mediocre news to younger generations.

How older Christians explain the gospel often attempts to answer questions Millennials and teens just aren't asking. Previous generations asked questions like "How do I get to heaven?" or "What do I do with my guilt?" while younger generations ask entirely different questions, like "What does it mean for me to thrive as a human being?"

A couple of factors influence this shift. One is anxiety. Millennials and Gen Z have higher levels of anxiety than any other generation. According to Dr. Betsy Nesbit, such high levels of anxiety put them in a constant state of "fight or flight"—and as a result, young people have a hard time thinking too far in the future. Like a hiker in front of a bear who's not thinking about that project due next week or their plans for retirement, for many young people questions like "What happens after I die?" simply aren't relevant. Yet.

A second reason they are asking different questions is that Western culture is slowly making a shift from a guilt-and-innocence culture to a shame-and-honor culture. The difference between shame and guilt is subtle yet profound. If you make a mistake in a guilt culture, it's just that: a mistake. If you make a mistake in a shame culture, *you* are the mistake.

A shame culture asks different questions from a guilt culture—and the gospel speaks differently to a shame culture than it does to a guilt culture. Teens and young adults are asking where they belong, how they are significant, how to deal with anxiety, what to do with their loneliness.

If our gospel can't answer those questions, it doesn't feel like good news. On the other hand, if it *does* answer those longings, they will be much more likely to receive it—and share with others how God has impacted their lives.

Q *How can church leaders help remove barriers so that young people can consider and share the gospel?*

A Church leaders need to release the assumption that the gospel that was good news to older generations is the entirety of the gospel. Have we been presenting the message of Jesus in its biblical and historical fullness? Arguably not. The gospel is robust enough to be good news to every generation.

> Church leaders need to release the assumption that the gospel that was good news to older generations is the entirety of the gospel

If our only understanding or expression of salvation is what happens after we die, then our message will not be perceived as relevant to most younger people. But when Jesus talks about being saved in the Gospels, he frequently is talking about *right now*, not the "after you die" that characterizes some older generations' gospel presentations. It's notable that the Greek word for the word "saved" is the word *sozo*, which does means to be saved, but also means to become whole. What I find fascinating is that when Jesus says, "Your faith has *saved* you," the word is *sozo*— and when he heals someone and says, "Your faith has made you *well*," the word is *also sozo*. This is a balanced, full understanding of what the good news is doing.

For Millennials and Gen Z, the good news of the gospel is that salvation is not only for later, it is something that is happening *now*—without diminishing the importance of "later." Jesus wants us to experience wholeness *now*—physically, spiritually, emotionally and relationally. So when it comes to their felt needs, we need to offer young people more than just platitudes or future promises. We need to walk them through the hard work of spiritual formation and an invitation to experience the power of the Holy Spirit. Right now.

Similar is the topic of sin. If the young are increasingly shaped by a shame culture, then when we talk about sin and how God hates it, we inadvertently communicate that *they* are unwanted or rejected by God. This could not be further from the truth. It's important that we reframe sin for this generation in a way that is theologically correct, but also that proactively communicates God's love for people. God hates sin because he loves us so much that he can't stand to see us finding "life" where there is no life. This explanation provokes the question from someone who hears it: "If there is no life in the things I do, then where is there life?" That's a good-news question, and it flies with young people.

For teens and young adults, compassion—not judgment—is the starting place of the gospel.

If we are serious about reaching new generations, we need to be willing to challenge our assumptions about what the gospel is. We also need to engage people out of compassion and love rather than judgment, because it is the kindness of the Lord that leads to repentance. If we can communicate and reflect a Jesus who loves them and meets their greatest felt needs, I believe many young people will decide to follow Jesus—and share a vibrant faith with coming generations. *

Qualities of a Good Person to Talk with About Faith

% among US adults; respondents could select all that apply.

Non-Christians / lapsed Christians
- ● Someone I would talk to about faith
- ● Christians I know

Practicing Christians
- ● Someone who is gifted at sharing their faith
- ● Completely true of me

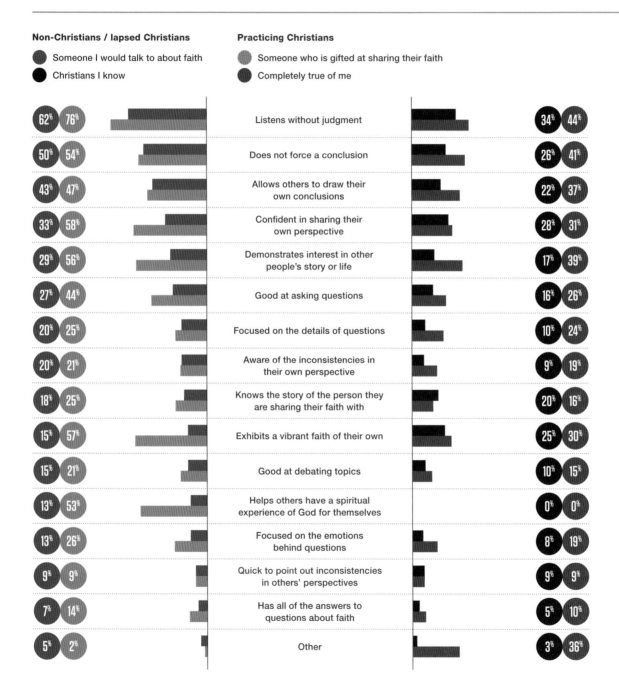

Non-Christians / lapsed Christians		Quality	Practicing Christians	
62%	76%	Listens without judgment	34%	44%
50%	54%	Does not force a conclusion	26%	41%
43%	47%	Allows others to draw their own conclusions	22%	37%
33%	58%	Confident in sharing their own perspective	28%	31%
29%	56%	Demonstrates interest in other people's story or life	17%	39%
27%	44%	Good at asking questions	16%	26%
20%	25%	Focused on the details of questions	10%	24%
20%	21%	Aware of the inconsistencies in their own perspective	9%	19%
18%	25%	Knows the story of the person they are sharing their faith with	20%	16%
15%	57%	Exhibits a vibrant faith of their own	25%	30%
15%	21%	Good at debating topics	10%	15%
13%	53%	Helps others have a spiritual experience of God for themselves	0%	0%
13%	26%	Focused on the emotions behind questions	8%	19%
9%	9%	Quick to point out inconsistencies in others' perspectives	9%	9%
7%	14%	Has all of the answers to questions about faith	5%	10%
5%	2%	Other	3%	36%

REVIVING EVANGELISM *n=1,993 US adults 18 and older, May 2018.*

Christians Aren't Clear on What "Works"

Many practicing Christians overestimate the importance of their personal virtues when it comes to non-Christians' receptivity to the gospel message. And they tend to downplay the significance of factors that are largely beyond their individual control, such as Christianity's overall reputation and reasonable evidence for faith in Christ.

Practicing Christians' ideas about what is most important to people considering Christianity do not always match up with reality (see p. 56). Non-Christians are most concerned with the evidence for Christianity and the overall reputation of the faith, while practicing Christians think a firsthand spiritual experience is the most salient factor. (What practicing Christians perceive about non-Christians is actually closer to lapsed Christians' priorities.)

A plurality of non-Christians wishes for credible, reasonable explanations of the Christian faith, to see elements of proof for its claims (44%). This does not necessarily mean Christians should invest heavily in traditional apologetics, however. As demonstrated by non-Christians' distaste for street preaching and tracts, depersonalized outreach that feels intrusive or manipulative is likely to lower openness to the gospel rather than encourage its further consideration. (See the Q&A with Michelle Jones, p. 26, for additional insights on evidence and authenticity.)

The tarnished reputation of Christianity is likewise a barrier for about one-third of non-Christians (34%) and one in five lapsed Christians (21%). Those who want to give others an opportunity to connect with Jesus struggle uphill against the weight of a Christianity perceived as beholden to political power, hypocritical on issues of sexual integrity and as a system that protects troubling public figures. Practicing Christians need to grapple with how the overall reputation of the faith may impact their personal witness.

Supporting evidence for faith is important to some lapsed Christians, but they differ from non-Christians in a few notable ways that

Non-Christians want credible, reasonable explanations of the Christian faith, to see elements of proof for its claims—but depersonalized outreach lowers openness to the gospel

Factors That Could Increase Interest in Christianity

% among US adults 18 and older; respondents could select up to three.

n=942 US adults 18 and older who are not practicing Christians and are not interested in Christianity, May 2018; n=781 US practicing Christians 18 and older who say non-Christians are not interested in Christianity, May 2018.

● Non-Christians   ● Lapsed Christians   ● Practicing Christians' expectations

Factor	Non-Christians	Lapsed Christians	Practicing Christians' expectations
Christianity had better evidence to support it	44%	21%	14%
Christianity had a better reputation	34%	21%	23%
The Christians I know were more humble and aware of their shortcomings	28%	31%	33%
I had an eye-opening spiritual experience myself	28%	32%	40%
I saw various churches in my community working together more	24%	31%	27%
The Christians I know had better answers to my questions	19%	25%	21%
The Christians I know were more welcoming and hospitable	18%	26%	34%
The Christians I know were more open to outsiders	18%	19%	24%
The Christians I know were more open to my questions	16	19%	20%
The Christians I know cared more about me	14%	17%	29%
The Christians I know demonstrated a more vibrant personal faith	12%	14%	36%
The Christians I know were more articulate about their faith	11%	14%	18%
I knew more Christians to talk to about their faith	11%	21%	21%
Other	24%	11%	3%

may indicate the impact of past church experiences on their present lack of spiritual investment. For many, a revelatory spiritual experience would spark greater interest in faith (likely indicating a lack of such an experience in the past), alongside more unity and humility on the part of Christians (suggesting these qualities have not defined their past experience).

What about some of the common faith-sharing approaches taken by Christians? Which, if any, are people most open to? It depends.

One of the largest factors at play appears to be one's spiritual inclination (see p. 58). Non-Christians and lapsed Christians who say spirituality plays a significant role in their life, and those who say they have unanswered spiritual questions, tend to be more open to a variety of settings to explore questions of faith—while those who say otherwise are less open. For example, three in 10 of all non-Christians and lapsed Christians say they prefer a "casual, one-on-one conversation" (30%). But the percentage is higher among those for whom spirituality is significant (40%) than among those for whom it is not (27%). Similarly, people who agree strongly that they have unanswered spiritual questions are more likely to say they prefer one-on-one conversation (45%) than those who don't have such questions (20%).

Overall, settings that prioritize relational interactions tend to be more attractive than approaches that don't, even among those who are inclined to spirituality. Being approached by a street evangelist or with a tract, for example, are unpopular even with people who are already open to exploring faith—and among those who are not, such approaches may do more harm than good. Two-thirds of non-Christians who say spirituality plays "no role" in their lives select "none of the above" (64%).

Only about half say they have had at least one conversation with a Christian about faith or their beliefs during the past year (52%), but the vast majority have had at least one at some point in the past. Unsurprisingly, past negative interactions with a Christian significantly depress openness to exploring questions of faith. Sixty-two percent

People with unanswered spiritual questions tend to be more open to exploring faith

How People Would Like to Explore Faith

% among US non-Christians and lapsed Christians 18 and older

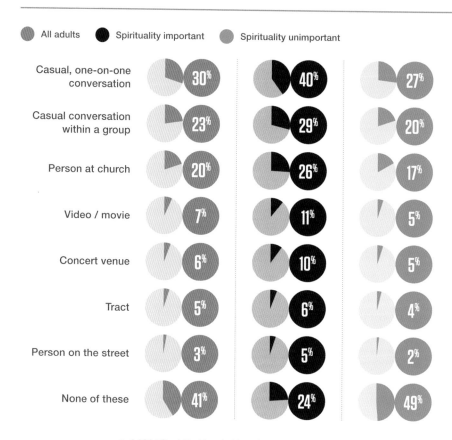

All adults ● Spirituality important ● Spirituality unimportant

	All adults	Spirituality important	Spirituality unimportant
Casual, one-on-one conversation	30%	40%	27%
Casual conversation within a group	23%	29%	20%
Person at church	20%	26%	17%
Video / movie	7%	11%	5%
Concert venue	6%	10%	5%
Tract	5%	6%	4%
Person on the street	3%	5%	2%
None of these	41%	24%	49%

n=1,001 US adults 18 and older who are not practicing Christians; May 2018.

of those who report having had negative interactions say no options interest them, compared to 40 percent of those with mixed interactions and 30 percent of those with positive interactions.

While further study is needed to make clear links between more difficult or challenging life circumstances and openness to exploring faith questions, there does seem to be a correlation between aspects of privilege experienced by non-Christians (such as majority ethnicity and higher income) and being *less* open to exploring faith. In general, people of color and adults with lower income tend to be more open than white and high-income Americans. It is worth remembering that the early explosive evangelistic success of Christianity was among the most socially marginalized—to the point that early pagans dismissed it as a fad appealing to those not welcome in polite society. It may be that the good news of Christ, today as in ancient times, sounds best to those who recognize they are most in need of it.

The Holy Spirit can, of course, use any means to draw people to Jesus. Few of us, regardless of social status, can predict what will inspire transformation in our lives. Stories abound of people who have heard and believed in the message of Jesus through the most

· · · · · · · · · · · · · · · ·

In addition to how they would *like* to explore questions of faith, researchers also asked non-Christians and lapsed Christians about how they *have experienced* evangelism. Their experiences with tracts and being approached by someone on the street suggest one reason some reject depersonalized methods of sharing faith: because they have experienced those methods and didn't like it.

How People Have Experienced Evangelism
% among US non-Christians and lapsed Christians 18 and older

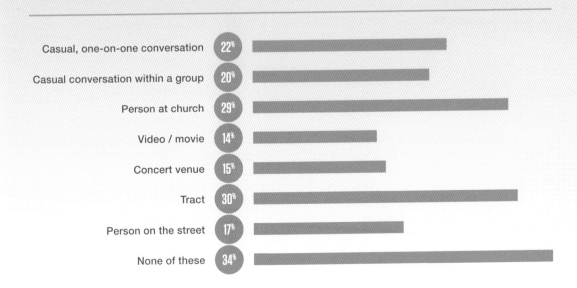

Casual, one-on-one conversation	22%
Casual conversation within a group	20%
Person at church	29%
Video / movie	14%
Concert venue	15%
Tract	30%
Person on the street	17%
None of these	34%

n=1,001 US adults 18 and older who are not practicing Christians; May 2018.

unlikely of encounters. True as that is, it appears non-Christians look most favorably on approaches that spark sincere, friendly engagement.

That is good news, because many Christians have similar preferences (see below). Most favor small settings to share their faith—one on one or in small groups. There are, of course, a handful Christians who evangelize from a stadium stage, but that doesn't reflect most people's reality: fulfilling the mission of Christ in small, relational ways.

There are real opportunities for Christians who want to share the good news of Jesus. Let's look at a few of them. ✳

How Christians Are Most Comfortable Sharing Faith
% "completely comfortable" among US practicing Christians 18 and older

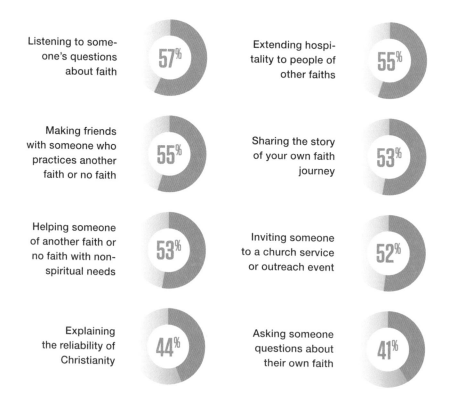

Listening to someone's questions about faith — **57%**

Extending hospitality to people of other faiths — **55%**

Making friends with someone who practices another faith or no faith — **55%**

Sharing the story of your own faith journey — **53%**

Helping someone of another faith or no faith with non-spiritual needs — **53%**

Inviting someone to a church service or outreach event — **52%**

Explaining the reliability of Christianity — **44%**

Asking someone questions about their own faith — **41%**

n=992 US practicing Christians 18 and older; May 2018.

CHALLENGES & OPPORTUNITIES FOR SHARING FAITH TODAY
Q&A with Mary Healy

Dr. Mary Healy, Professor of Scripture at Sacred Heart Major Seminary in Detroit, is a bestselling author and international speaker. She is a general editor of the Catholic Commentary on Sacred Scripture *and author of two of its volumes,* The Gospel of Mark *and* Hebrews. *Her other books include* The Spiritual Gifts Handbook *and* Healing: Bringing the Gift of God's Mercy to the World. *She was appointed by Pope Francis as one of the first three women ever to serve on the Pontifical Biblical Commission.*

Q *What are the most pressing cultural challenges to evangelization that you encounter?*

A I'd like to mention three. First, radical secularism. It's done deep damage to the human spirit. Many people in our time are affected by a kind of spiritual numbness. Beginning from childhood, they've been overstimulated, over-scheduled, over-indulged and over-exposed to sexual content. They've been taught that self-fulfillment, sexual freedom and economic success are the highest values. So they often seem to have lost interest in the most important questions of life: Why do I exist? What is my mission in life and how do I fulfill it? What is true love and how do I find it? Many people today show indifference to these deeper questions. But no matter what, those questions are there beneath the surface.

Second, many people are carrying deep inner wounds, whether due to family breakdown, sexual exploitation or the shallowness of screen-based relationships. There can be a hidden fear of allowing God in and letting wounds be exposed. But this challenge becomes an opportunity! When people begin to sense the emptiness of contemporary secular culture, they seek for something more. And when they discover Jesus can heal the deepest wounds of their heart, they begin to open themselves to his grace.

A third big challenge is that people have been fed the absurd myth that there is a conflict between science and religion, between reason and Christian faith. Of course the opposite is true: Christianity, and in particular the Catholic Church, has been the greatest promoter of science and the champion of reason, while at the same time recognizing the limitations of reason. People need and deserve to hear the solid reasons for Christian faith. People need to know that believing in Christ does not mean becoming irrational, but discovering the great fulfillment of human reason.

Believing in Christ does not mean becoming irrational, but discovering the great fulfillment of human reason

Q **What are the unique opportunities for sharing faith that we can maximize today? What have you seen draw people to Christ?**

A There's no replacement for a real encounter with God's power and the holiness of his people. What is immensely effective in evangelization is a return to the original "method" that Jesus himself used and commanded his disciples to use: proclaiming the gospel accompanied by healings and miracles. These are the Lord's "audiovisual aids" by which he confirms the truth of the message. I've seen again and again that when we are willing to take risks in faith as we evangelize, the Lord backs us up through the power of the Holy Spirit. The gospel is a message in words that addresses the human being's capacity for truth, but it is also a message of power that brings people into a personal encounter with Jesus.

Also indispensable and non-negotiable in evangelization is the witness of a holy life. Even though the world makes fun of holiness, in reality, holiness has never lost its attractiveness. Especially today in our narcissistic culture, getting to know a person who is authentically self-giving, pure-hearted, humble, prayerful, joyful and in love with Jesus can be transformative. Personal holiness is a compelling testimony to the truth of the gospel.

Q *How can Christians of varying backgrounds unite in service of a wider commitment to sharing and living out the gospel of Jesus?*

A As Pope John Paul II wrote, "What unites us is much greater than what divides us." Yes, there are very real and significant theological differences that cannot be papered over, but unity will come first and foremost through prayer and deeper conversion to Christ on the part of every Christian.

As a Catholic, I am thrilled if an evangelical or Pentecostal brings a secular person to faith in Christ and membership in their church. They have brought a lost sinner home to God! I hope that they would think the same way about Catholic evangelization. Our goal is the same: to fulfill Jesus' commission to go and make disciples of all nations. So we should look for creative ways to partner in evangelization and works of charity. An area of immense potential for collaboration is the arts and tech—film, drama, painting, literature, music and the internet.

Q *A sense of negative Church reputation holds back many non-Christians from considering Christian faith. How can we navigate that reality and move the gospel forward?*

A The fact that the crimes and cover-ups of more than a few church leaders have made headlines around the world, causing countless people to be repelled by the Church, is a source of unspeakable grief for Catholics. Yet the Lord is using this crisis. Catholics have sometimes tended to focus too much on the Church and too little on Jesus. Our evangelization has at times been Church-centric instead of Christocentric.

As Cardinal Avery Dulles once wrote, "The Church has one inescapable task: to lift up Christ. When she seeks to lift herself up, the Church becomes weak, but when she acknowledges her own weakness and proclaims her Lord, she is strong." And St. Paul reminds us, "What we preach is not ourselves, but *Jesus Christ as Lord*, with ourselves as your servants for Jesus' sake" (2 Cor 4:5). The crisis is helping us correct these theological distortions and place our full focus where it needs to be: on Jesus our crucified and risen Lord, the only one who can fulfill the deepest longings of the human heart.

So the best way for us to navigate this situation is to be honest, to disavow any kind of triumphalism and to admit the Church is filled with fallen human beings. We are truly a hospital for sinners.

Even our shepherds may fail us, sometimes horrendously. It is not the first time and will not be the last. But our faith is not in them. It is in him. Jesus the Lord is in the Church, and despite all its failures he continues to give himself to us in the sacraments and to pour out rivers of grace and mercy on all who come to him. ✳

3 FERTILE SOIL

In the natural world, change—however drastic—is accompanied by opportunity. Even the devastation of a wildfire or volcanic eruption creates the conditions for ecosystems to rebound and flourish. Ecologists tell us of certain trees in the Western United States whose seeds can only germinate in the conditions following a forest fire, or of the soil "reset" that accompanies a landslide or heavy flooding. In nature, change—even change that is threatening or catastrophic for an existing system—is a powerful cultivator of life.

In this sense, for all the seeming loss of ground in evangelistic culture and practice, the *Reviving Evangelism* data indicate significant hope for the Christian community's stewardship of the gospel message.

But flourishing in change requires adaptation. If American Christians can respond with agility to today's challenges while retaining their core distinctiveness and message, the gospel will take root, no matter the culture's trajectory. But if hard realities are ignored, it's difficult to imagine evangelistic success in a culture no longer inclined to see faith as compelling or relevant.

In this chapter, we examine standout examples of that hope, and begin to consider how Christians can respond to an invitation to flourish and share faith in a new environment.

> *The data indicate hope for the Christian community's stewardship of the gospel*

· · · · · · · · · · · · · · · · · · · ·

NON-CHRISTIANS LIKE CHRISTIANS MORE THAN CHRISTIANITY

Christianity's reputation has taken some damaging hits in recent years. Across the board, non-Christians think more highly of the Christians they personally know than of "Christianity" as a whole. Even atheists and agnostics, who tend to be most skeptical of (or even hostile toward) Christianity, have a higher opinion of individual Christians than of the faith overall.

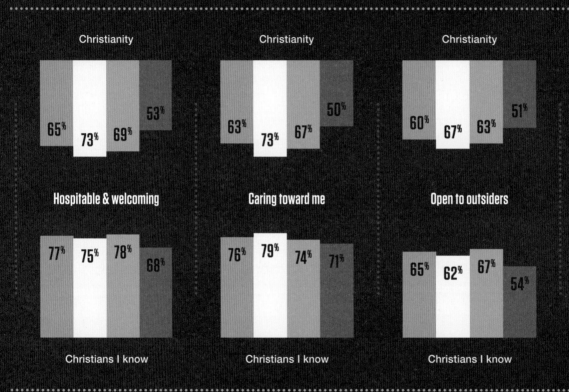

Christianity

65% 73% 69% 53%

Hospitable & welcoming

77% 75% 78% 68%

Christians I know

Christianity

63% 73% 67% 50%

Caring toward me

76% 79% 74% 71%

Christians I know

Christianity

60% 67% 63% 51%

Open to outsiders

65% 62% 67% 54%

Christians I know

... STILL, MORE THAN 1 IN 5 EXPRESSES INTEREST IN EXPLORING THE CHRISTIAN FAITH

I am interested in learning more about Christianity and what it could mean for my life

 22%

 29%

8%

 32%

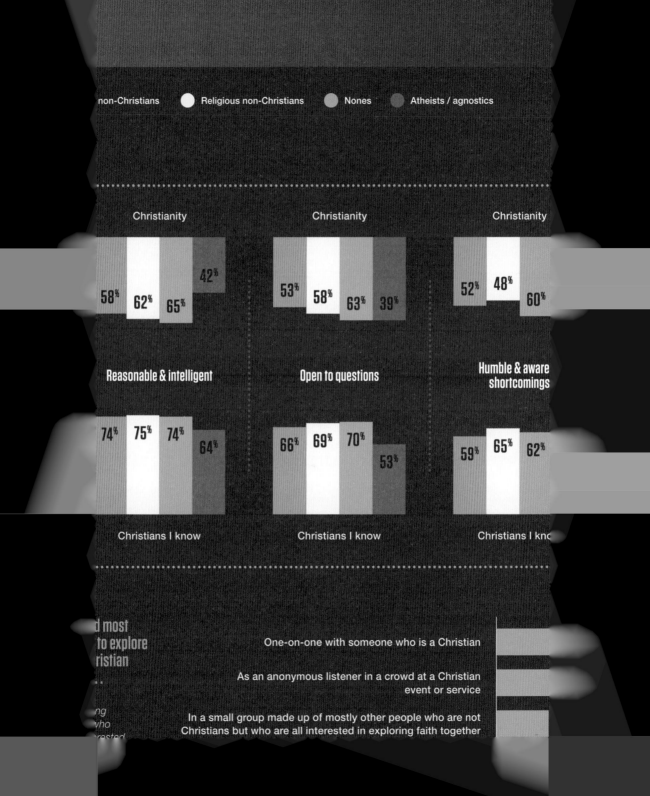

Christianity

Christianity

Christianity

58% 62% 65% 42%

53% 58% 63% 39%

52% 48% 60%

Reasonable & intelligent

Open to questions

Humble & aware shortcomings

74% 75% 74% 64%

66% 69% 70% 53%

59% 65% 62%

Christians I know

Christians I know

Christians I kn

d most
to explore
ristian

One-on-one with someone who is a Christian

As an anonymous listener in a crowd at a Christian
event or service

ng
who
rested

In a small group made up of mostly other people who are not
Christians but who are all interested in exploring faith together

YOUNG NON-CHRISTIANS TALK ABOUT SPIRITUAL MATTERS A LOT MORE THAN OLDER ADULTS

Millennials report many more faith conversations and evangelistic encounters than older non-Christians. This is partly due to greater religious diversity among their family and friends—but that's not the whole story. For at least some young adults, there appears to be greater curiosity about spirituality and, specifically, deeper interest in Christianity.

● Millennial non-Christians   ● All older non-Christians

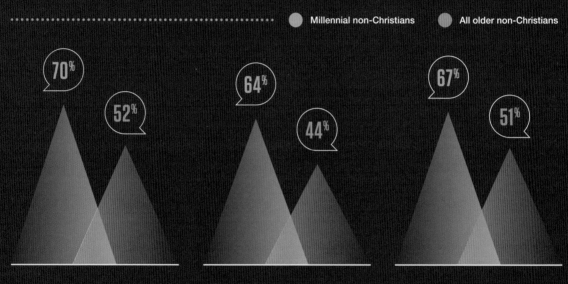

70%	52%

I have had one or more conversations about my faith perspectives or beliefs with a close friend or family member of a different faith in the past year

64%	44%

I have had one or more conversations about my faith perspectives or beliefs with a practicing Christian in the past year

67%	51%

A Christian has tried to share his or her faith with me one or more times in the past year

. . . AND ARE TWICE AS LIKELY TO EXPRESS PERSONAL INTEREST IN CHRISTIANITY

I am interested in learning more about Christianity and what it could mean for my life

Millennial non-Christians   **36%**

All older non-Christians

16%

Evangelistic methods I have experienced

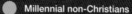 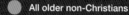

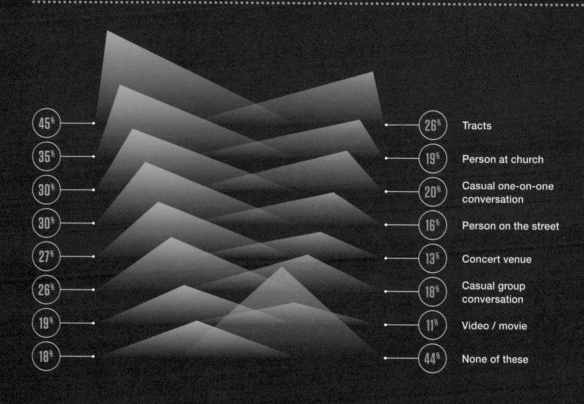

Millennial	All older	Method
45%	26%	Tracts
35%	19%	Person at church
30%	20%	Casual one-on-one conversation
30%	16%	Person on the street
27%	13%	Concert venue
26%	18%	Casual group conversation
19%	11%	Video / movie
18%	44%	None of these

I would most prefer to explore the Christian faith …

% among those who are interested

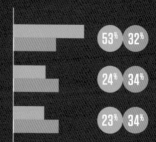

	Millennial	All older
One-on-one with someone who is a Christian	53%	32%
As an anonymous listener in a crowd at a Christian event or service	24%	34%
In a small group made up of mostly other people who are not Christians but who are all interested in exploring faith together	23%	34%

n=620 US non-Christians 18 and older; May 2018

Demographics Aren't Destiny, but Sometimes They Help

Demographic factors are many, but analysts note four of particular weight in this study: current faith, an urban setting, income level and generation. Because these factors change slowly (or not at all) for most individuals and communities, they represent a unique strategic opportunity for gospel-sharing also to evolve slowly.

Religious Non-Christians

The greatest sense of being on a spiritual quest is found among currently-practicing religious non-Christians—a group consisting primarily of Muslims, Hindus and Buddhists—and those who were raised in those faiths but are not currently religious. Two-thirds of respondents connected to a religion other than Christianity indicate some level of spiritual hunger (68%). That's less than the three-quarters of practicing Christians who say so (77%), but significantly more than the three in 10 lapsed Christians and religiously unaffiliated non-Christians (29%) who say they are on such a quest.

This signal of openness is an opportunity. Getting to know neighbors or co-workers who come from non-Christian religious backgrounds introduces Christians to people different from them but who share a higher-than-average interest in spirituality. As we've seen, Millennials are more likely to already have such friendships, compared with older Christians—so Gen X, Boomer and Elder believers may need to step out of their everyday zone of comfort to establish new relationships.

Christian leaders, such as local pastors, might consider building positive relationships with leaders of other religious communities and even joining forces with them to serve shared neighborhoods. Spiritual hunger is contagious, so cultivating an ethos of spiritual questing across faith communities could have a snowball effect to produce opportunities for gospel engagement.

Two-thirds of non-Christians connected to a religion other than Christianity indicate some level of spiritual hunger

Spiritual Mindsets of Religious Non-Christians

% strongly + somewhat agree among US adults

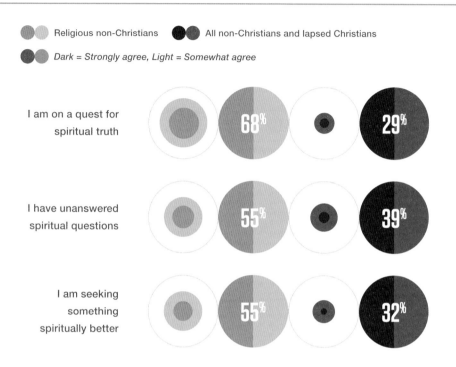

Religious non-Christians   •   All non-Christians and lapsed Christians

Dark = Strongly agree, Light = Somewhat agree

I am on a quest for spiritual truth — **68%** / **29%**

I have unanswered spiritual questions — **55%** / **39%**

I am seeking something spiritually better — **55%** / **32%**

n=1,001 US adults 18 and older who are not practicing Christians; May 2018.

Urban Dwellers

As noted earlier, adults in urban environments tend to exhibit higher levels of spiritual hunger and general openness to evangelistic methods, compared to people in the suburbs, small towns or rural settings. Whatever the reasons for this "urban openness," it constitutes an opportunity for Christians in high-density and high-diversity communities to consider how to respond with gospel intention. Does your church community reflect the diversity of age, ethnicity and gender in your neighborhood? If not, why not? What can you do differently to connect with people who surround you on a daily basis?

Urban & Open

· · · · · · · · · · · · · · · · · · · ·

City-dwelling non-Christians tend to be more spiritually open compared to those in the suburbs or rural communities, and practicing Christians in the city tend to be more comfortable talking about their faith compared to their sisters and brothers elsewhere. It may be that the dense urban fabric of cities fosters the relational skills necessary for engaging with people different from oneself.

How can Christian leaders in the city use this existing dynamic to encourage urban Christians to reach out in their everyday lives? And how can suburban and rural leaders help to weave a denser social fabric that builds relational skills and habits of engagement in Christians eager to share their faith?

Christians who are *not* urban dwellers must do some soul-searching, as well. What about city living can kindle spiritual interest? What might be done in your suburb or small town to create similar dynamics?

The data indicate, generally speaking, higher spiritual hunger among ethnic minorities than among white adults. There is some crossover here between ethnicity and urban living—though, obviously, many people of color live in suburbs and rural areas, and many white people live in cities. But it is worth considering how greater ethnic diversity might raise the spiritual temperature of a given community.

People with Low Income

Adults who report an annual household income of less than $50K seem to be more aware of their spiritual hunger than those who earn more, regardless of ethnicity. Certainly they are more likely to agree that they have "unanswered spiritual questions" and that "something feels missing from my life" (see p. 78).

Christianity's message of hope has always uniquely impacted the poor, and the high level of spiritual openness among lower-income Americans constitutes a real invitation. Amid cultural prejudice against and frequent marginalization of the poor and disadvantaged, Christianity stresses the inestimable value and shared humanity of all persons, and beckons them all to a kingdom where the last will be first—a kingdom that poor people often seem to yearn for more deeply than their richer neighbors.

Spiritual Mindsets of Urban Non-Christians & Lapsed Christians

% strongly + somewhat agree among US adults

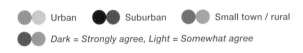

Urban   Suburban   Small town / rural

Dark = Strongly agree, Light = Somewhat agree

I have unanswered spiritual questions

47%   36%   38%

I am seeking something spiritually better

39%   30%   29%

I am on a quest for spiritual truth

38%   25%   26%

n=1,001 US adults 18 and older who are not practicing Christians; May 2018.

ON RELATING WELL
Q&A with Rufus Smith

Rev. Rufus Smith IV is senior pastor of Hope Evangelical Presbyterian Church, a large multiethnic congregation in Memphis, Tennessee, and founder of the Memphis Christian Pastors' Network, a clergy-only network to bridge the "trust gap" between ethnically and denominationally diverse pastors. Rev. Smith has been married to Jacqueline for 34 years, and together they have three adult children.

Q *What skills must Christians develop to effectively share their faith?*

A We need to learn to look more like Jesus, our benchmark for evangelism. In John 4:1–24 we find that Jesus, a Jew, shared the good news across racial, cultural, historical and gender divides in conversation with a Samaritan woman. From that encounter we can learn at least two relational skills from the master teacher.

First, we learn that *there is no impact without contact*. Jesus-followers must be willing to venture into the territory of the unchurched, de-churched, over-churched or the "religiously unaffiliated." We must go to them rather than waiting for them to come to us. Jesus broke protocol by going into Samaria, a region that was geographically proximate but culturally distant to what was "home" for Jesus. But he was teaching his disciples (and consequently us) that, if we want to enlarge the kingdom of God, we must move from familiar circles of contact to unfamiliar territory. (And be enriched in the good news ourselves, by the way.)

As a pastor, my world is saturated with church and the churched. That means I am constantly challenged—and often fail—to initiate contact with those who live in another "world." When I get it right, I do this in various ways: through non-church sports leagues, public school volunteering, Toastmasters and other social clubs. That contact keeps me connected—and every Christian needs it.

Second, *there is no information without real conversation*.

In the story, notice that Jesus asked the Samaritan woman a question: "May I have a drink of water?" That sparked a follow-up question ("Where is your husband?"), which sparked a deeper conversation. I think it behooves us as Jesus-followers to be more Socratic (engaging in dialog) and less didactic (giving people advice or information). The relational skill of *conversation*, as modeled by Jesus, encourages openness and connection, not only in gospel sharing but also in every arena of life. It bonds us together, which creates a rich setting for sharing the gospel.

Q ***What assumptions hold us back from rich relationships?***

A Largely, how we think of other people. Our inaccurate generalizations, as well as simple ignorance, rob us of the possibility of rich, God-ordained relationships with those different from us, especially those outside the Christian faith. We are over-saturated

The relational skill of conversation, as modeled by Jesus, encourages openness and connection

with audiovisual media and extensive messaging that subliminally leads us to make sweeping generalizations about people and entire groups: "rich," "poor," "them," "us" and a host of other barriers, real and imagined. These generalizations are exacerbated by ignorance, which breeds fear, and often are paired with residential separation, which reinforces stereotypes. All this contributes to a weak social fabric that discourages us from getting to know each other and sharing the message of Jesus.

Q ***What has your church learned about fostering rich relationship?***

A We are learning so much. In our church we have sought and fought to combat generalizations and ignorance through a course called Ethnos. It's a 10-week covenant to explore and experience other cultures for two hours once a week. Eighteen to 24 persons of diverse ethnicity and age sign an agreement to commit and are pre-assigned to tables of six for the duration of the course. They listen to each other and engage in three spiritual "adventures" outside of the class with each other. The point is to intentionally practice the skills that make for a bonded, rich community.

It was there that Roosevelt met Stephen. The former was black, the latter was white. One liked rhythm and blues, one classical music. One was an engineer, the other a physician. One was discriminated against here in Memphis because of the color of his skin, the other was not. Both were Baby Boomers but from two different worlds. Both made wrong assumptions and fostered ignorance toward the other "type" of person.

But each was also curious—and a Jesus-follower. During Ethnos, Roosevelt and Stephen spent 10 consecutive Thursday nights together. They and their other four tablemates ate 10 meals together. They studied Bible teaching on "loving our neighbors as

Our inaccurate generalizations rob us of the possibility of rich, God-ordained relationships with those different from us

ourselves" together. They engaged in candid conversation together. They watched an assigned movie in one of their homes together. They participated in three spiritual adventures outside of the classroom together. They graduated together.

And they forged a four-year friendship that only ended when Stephen died unexpectedly from an asthmatic attack while vacationing with his wife. Roosevelt, Stephen's friend, was one of three eulogists at his funeral. What had made the difference?

Experiencing the gospel. *Together*. ✳

Spiritual Mindsets of Low-Income Non-Christians & Lapsed Christians

% strongly + somewhat agree among US adults

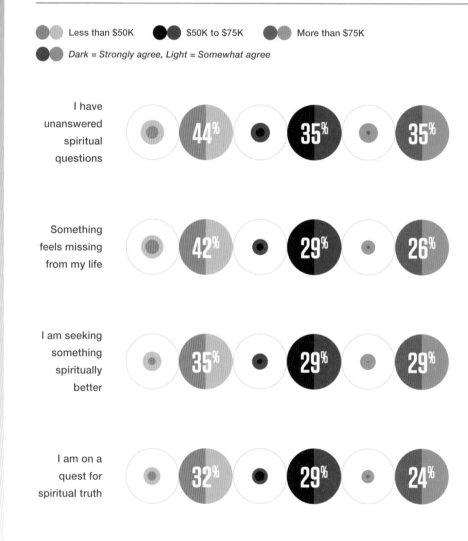

● ● Less than $50K ● ● $50K to $75K ● ● More than $75K

● ● *Dark = Strongly agree, Light = Somewhat agree*

I have unanswered spiritual questions
44% 35% 35%

Something feels missing from my life
42% 29% 26%

I am seeking something spiritually better
35% 29% 29%

I am on a quest for spiritual truth
32% 29% 24%

n=1,001 US adults 18 and older who are not practicing Christians; May 2018.

But sharing good news with the poor is not only good for the poor. As Barna found in research among UK and US adults, published in *Christians Who Make a Difference*, caring for people in poverty strongly correlates to deeper discipleship engagement. Churchgoers who prioritize care for and action on behalf of poor people also love Jesus, trust the scriptures, seek to honor God with their lives and want to share their faith with others.

Young Adults

Asked to rate their agreement with the statements "I experience a general sense of emptiness" and "I often feel rejected," younger Americans are more apt than older adults to agree. There are little or no drastic differences between Millennial and older non-Christians when it comes to spiritual hunger and experiences—but on the question of feelings of emptiness and rejection, many young people, in contrast to older adults, clearly sense something is wrong. It is more common for them to admit experiencing some kind of relational struggle or inward discontent (see p. 80).

While it may seem heartless to welcome their inner emptiness, it's unavoidably true that really, deeply feeling one's spiritual need can open a door to meaningful conversation and an encounter with Jesus. Hurting, restless people find healing and rest in him—and it helps if they're looking. Many young adults, simply by virtue of being young, are more likely than older people to be in a "searching season" of life—for identity, for better answers—and therefore more open to change or transformation.

Good Conversation Makes People Hungry for More

Researchers asked people how many conversations about faith they have had in the past year, and discovered something interesting: A higher number of faith conversations correlates with a greater level of openness to exploring faith. Those who report having *no*

Nearly half of Millennials agree that "I experience a general sense of emptiness"

Feelings of Emptiness and Rejection, by Generation
% among US non-Christians and lapsed Christians

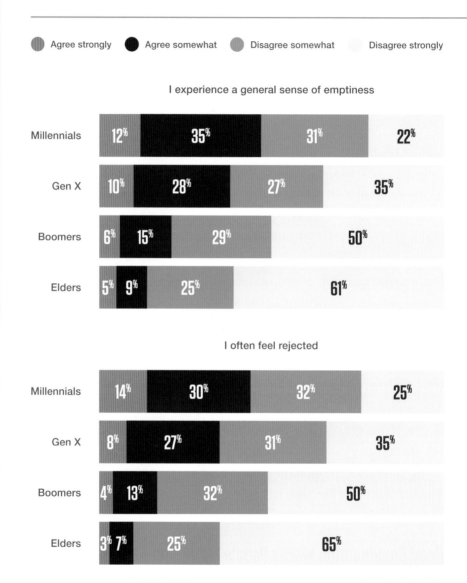

Legend: Agree strongly · Agree somewhat · Disagree somewhat · Disagree strongly

I experience a general sense of emptiness

Generation	Agree strongly	Agree somewhat	Disagree somewhat	Disagree strongly
Millennials	12%	35%	31%	22%
Gen X	10%	28%	27%	35%
Boomers	6%	15%	29%	50%
Elders	5%	9%	25%	61%

I often feel rejected

Generation	Agree strongly	Agree somewhat	Disagree somewhat	Disagree strongly
Millennials	14%	30%	32%	25%
Gen X	8%	27%	31%	35%
Boomers	4%	13%	32%	50%
Elders	3%	7%	25%	65%

n=1,001 US adults 18 and older who are not practicing Christians; May 2018.

conversations about spiritual matters are far more likely to say they would choose none of the possible avenues for faith exploration, while people who have had even a single conversation are more likely to choose another option.

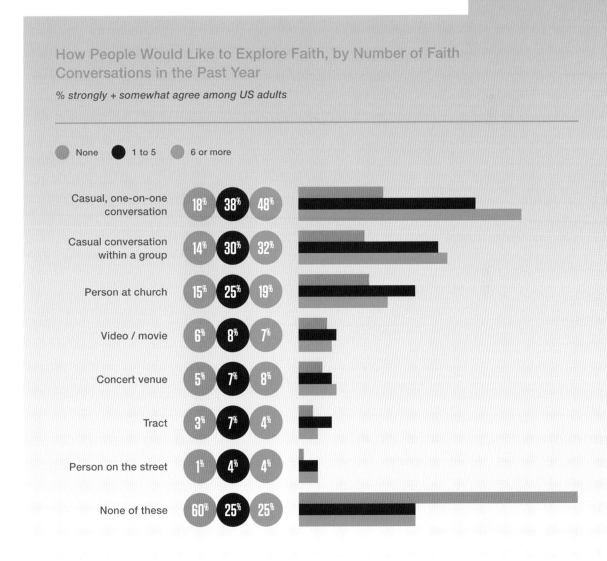

How People Would Like to Explore Faith, by Number of Faith Conversations in the Past Year

% strongly + somewhat agree among US adults

None • 1 to 5 • 6 or more

Casual, one-on-one conversation — 18% | 38% | 48%
Casual conversation within a group — 14% | 30% | 32%
Person at church — 15% | 25% | 19%
Video / movie — 6% | 8% | 7%
Concert venue — 5% | 7% | 8%
Tract — 3% | 7% | 4%
Person on the street — 1% | 4% | 4%
None of these — 60% | 25% | 25%

n=1,001 US adults 18 and older who are not practicing Christians; May 2018.

Spiritual Hunger Is Contagious

. . . .

Spiritual hunger is not static—and Christians can help it grow. The data indicates that spiritual hunger varies among non-Christians in part *depending on the Christians they know*. When non-Christians have experienced vibrancy, personal care, intelligence, reasonableness and a gentle, non-judgmental approach from Christians, their spiritual curiosity overall and their interest in Christianity specifically are elevated.

This implies that spiritual hunger has a social element. We all play a part in encouraging or depressing the spiritual hunger of our neighbors.

It could be that bringing a spiritual element into secularized spaces is refreshing, giving people language to better name a struggle or experience. To use the example of meditation-turned-mindfulness, a non-Christian who senses there is something more happening when they quiet themselves may be surprised to learn there is a rich Christian tradition of meditation that names their experience in a richer and more holistic way than mere "mindfulness." They may leave the conversation with a new level of curiosity, respect and openness—and feeling validated in their spiritual experience by a Christian.

On that point, it's vital for Christians to remember there are two sides to every conversation. Listening to and expressing empathy for non-Christians' experiences will help to ensure spiritual conversation has a lasting and positive impact. ✳

PUTTING THE "GOOD" BACK IN GOOD NEWS
Q&A with Kevin Palau

Kevin Palau is the son of international evangelist Luis Palau. He joined the Luis Palau Association (LPA) in 1985 and began directing day-to-day ministry operations in the late 1990s. Under his leadership, LPA has produced some of the largest Christian events ever staged, created a worldwide network of hundreds of partner evangelists and developed new models for citywide outreach that integrate major community service initiatives with open-air evangelistic gatherings. He lives in Beaverton, Oregon, with his wife, Michelle, and their three children.

Q *You have a unique window into global evangelism. What changes are you seeing in global culture with regard to sharing the gospel?*

A It varies widely based on context. In the US, Australia and most of Western Europe the challenge is inspiring Jesus followers to be bolder and more joyful in sharing faith. Many are discouraged and have become fearful to bear witness to what Christ has done in their lives, based on cultural pressures. (At the same time, there are encouraging signs: Many evangelists, including our team, are seeing larger crowds than ever gathering for evangelistic outreaches.) Alpha continues to bear fruit and the number of churches running it in the West continues to grow. Many cities are pursuing a "city gospel movement" approach, where Christians unite over the long haul, pursuing the good of their city in a holistic way that doesn't shy away from gospel-sharing.

God is always about the business of giving some of his people the gift of evangelism and, whether the times are fruitful or not, many will prayerfully seek new ways to share the Good News. As well, the harder things become in the West, the clearer the distinction will become between nominal, "cultural" Christians and those who are "all in."

In Latin America, Africa and many parts of Asia, it's harvest time! Many come to Christ daily all around the global south, and believers tend to be bold and joyful in sharing the good news.

Around the world, I'm seeing more evangelism cooperation between charismatic / Pentecostals and evangelicals than ever. Many within the Christian community (especially younger leaders) hunger for a faith that regularly experiences the supernatural, and a greater sense of spiritual authority, and in my experience this leads to bolder witness.

Q *Millennials are less committed than older Christians to the idea that "the best thing that could ever happen to someone is for them to come to know Jesus." Do you find a growing need to "evangelize" Christians on the importance of evangelism?*

A This is the key issue. If we believe the best thing that could happen to someone is to come to know and follow Jesus, then we *will* share our faith. If we lose that belief, we simply won't. And it seems like a growing number of Christians are unsure exactly how good the *good news* is.

The internet and social media make many believers feel cautious about saying what they believe and have experienced. There's a "practical universalism" that feels it's the height of arrogance to claim that Jesus is unique and that only in relationship with him can life be fully experienced. Christians can feel it.

We need to remind, encourage, equip, nudge and inspire Christians to care about evangelism. We do this by both celebrating and accelerating evangelism. Tell stories of those who come to Christ, and those who are attempting (sometimes with little or no visible success) to share their faith. If it's important to the local church then it should be celebrated in our services—and we should offer specific opportunities for everyday Christians to be trained in it. (Alpha is a great resource for this, in my experience.)

We must remind Christians that the good news is genuinely *good news*—for everybody to experience and everybody to share. We need to use those gifted in evangelism to remind and encourage the rest of us that sharing faith is an important part of being a faithful follower of Jesus. We must not divorce it from other aspects of discipleship, nor relegate evangelism to a role for "professional Christians."

Our hesitations are almost always related to fear: of failure, ridicule, being misunderstood. Fear of being lumped in with less-than-thoughtful or judgmental Christians who may confuse politics or social issues with the gospel.

Genuine spiritual renewal in the Holy Spirit is the best antidote to that fear. Where I've seen communities being renewed in their love for Jesus, I see a greater boldness and willingness to pray and share faith. We often get bogged down in concerns about methodology, which is seldom helpful. It's almost always a matter of our heart and will.

Younger leaders hunger for a faith that regularly experiences the supernatural

In Acts 2 and Acts 4, when the Holy Spirit comes in visible ways on the early group of Jesus followers, one of the clearest evidences is their boldness. Do we believe it's a privilege to share our faith? Are we confident that no matter how unprepared we feel, that if we are speaking well of Jesus we can trust God with the results?

Q **What practices should Christians foster to support evangelism?**

A Two come to mind: prayer and building community.

In prayer we seek to hear from God and align our heart and will to his. We can trust that since God is love, and since he sent his Son to be the savior of the world and to seek and save those who are lost, then the more time we spend with him in quiet prayer, interceding for those who we long to see come to know Christ, the more we will desire to share our faith.

Hospitality and building genuine community also further our witness. Anything that puts us into genuine relationships with those who don't already know Jesus is a good thing. We shouldn't feel it's inauthentic to seek opportunities to "use" such relational connections to share Jesus. If we genuinely believe our message is good news, isn't that exactly what we would do?

Serving others is a part of it. The Church always seems to need to relearn how to blend justice / service work with gospel proclamation. The pendulum swings from one emphasis to the other. Maintaining balance takes clear intention. The challenge here in the West is usually to inspire Jesus followers to be more willing to open their mouths in concert with living the good news. Right now, many Christians need to rediscover verbally sharing faith.

We don't have to lessen service to strengthen proclamation. We can be wildly enthusiastic about both! How we love others is part of sharing faith. It opens eyes and softens hearts. But too often

If we believe the best thing that could happen to someone is to come to know and follow Jesus, then we will share our faith

REVIVING EVANGELISM

Christians misuse the quote attributed to Saint Francis: "Preach the gospel at all times. When necessary, use words." Biblically, it is necessary to use words. We need them to convey the full truth, beauty and message of the Christian gospel. Evangelism happens in the broad context of life. How we love and serve our neighbors is a key part, but so is verbally bearing witness to Jesus and his life and work, and explicitly inviting others to join us.

A well-rounded understanding of the kingdom of God helps here. We have the immense privilege to join God in his work of renewing all things. This helps us see evangelism as more than saving individual souls. It's also about giving people the joy of joining the greatest movement in history. Salvation is personal. But it's also communal. It changes us and gives us hope, meaning and purpose. The gospel responds directly to the common challenges of our day. It's salvation for each of us and all of us. ✳

HEADWINDS: CHALLENGES FOR EVANGELISM

Barna highly values "seeing the whole" picture. A variety of factors has changed the landscape of evangelism, making it more complicated to share faith in Jesus with others. Here are some of the trends that constrain faith-sharing. (On the next page, you'll find unexpected shifts that empower the possibility of effective evangelism.)

Secular Rising

The increasing secular environment includes more religiously unaffiliated adults, especially among Millennials and Gen Z. Relatedly, we see a "secularizing the sacred" trend, which means religious language and meaning are being yanked from their sacred roots and grafted onto secular pursuits.

Belief in the Self

The vast majority of adults believes you find "truth" by looking inside yourself. In other words, people are shifting from *external* sources of authority—such as the Bible, the truth claims of Jesus and so on—to *internal* sources of authority.

Stay in Your Lane

More than four out of five Americans say one shouldn't criticize the life choices of others. So spiritual conversations—like telling someone they are in desperate, existential need of a Savior—face stiffer-than-ever social pressure not to offend.

Conversion = Extremism

In a lot of ways, attitudes toward Christianity are moving from being perceived as merely irrelevant to being viewed as extremist. For instance, three out of five adults (and 83% of non-Christians) believe trying to convert another person to their own faith is an example of religious extremism.

Bad Religion

Negative perceptions of Christianity are more entrenched in the general population—especially among non-Christians, and even more so among *young* non-Christians. Whether it's science vs. faith, a badly articulated position on sexuality or fallout from sex and abuse scandals, non-Christians can take their pick of reasons to write off the faith.

Skepticism of Sincerity

In the post-truth age, people are increasingly skeptical of sincerity and of certainty. Claims of fake news, spin and gloss make it harder to communicate heart to heart. Being earnest—really, really trying to convey a message from our deepest convictions—generates suspicion and, ironically, seems to lack credibility and authenticity.

Outsourcing Evangelism

Increasing numbers of Christians believe it is the responsibility of the local church—not their own job—to do the work of faith-sharing. In other words, the heavy lifting of spiritual conversations is being outsourced.

Conversational Barriers

Evangelicals have the highest self-reported levels of conversational barriers; that is, they struggle to have natural and normal conversations with people who are very different from themselves. Christians who are committed to sharing the good news of Jesus ought to be good at these kinds of conversations.

Not-So-Great Commission?

One of Barna's most surprising findings of recent years is the fact that 51% of Christian churchgoers say they have never heard of the concept of the Great Commission, reflecting a huge gap in awareness of one of the fundamental callings of every Christian: to make disciples.

Additional reading on these trends can be found in Spiritual Conversations in the Digital Age, *produced in partnership with Lutheran Hour Ministries;* Translating the Great Commission, *conducted in conjunction with Seed Company; and* Good Faith: Being a Christian When Society Thinks You're Irrelevant and Extreme *by David Kinnaman and Gabe Lyons.*

TAILWINDS: REVIVING EVANGELISM

We don't have to *like* the trends, but we do have to operate faithfully within our pressure-packed environment, especially by taking advantage of good things that are happening out there. Here are trends helping Christians create what's next when it comes to faith-sharing.

....

Radical Transparency

In Barna's early years, we had to tread carefully on what we asked and how we asked it. Sexuality was off limits. Queries on religion were subject to the "halo effect," as respondents often presented themselves as "Christian" and "religious." No more. Those social pressures are diminishing, revealing candid talk and a radically transparent landscape.

The Search for New Models

The current climate of skepticism—even among Christians—is forcing a hard look at what it takes to be effective at sharing the good news of Jesus. False notions of evangelistic impact are coming under greater scrutiny, which seems to spur fresh consideration of new (and not so new) models of evangelism.

Cultivating a New Mentality

Bringing people to the gospel requires a new mentality on the part of evangelists: that we are guides and conduits through which a sovereign God does his work. This means we can't assume things about what others are thinking or ram people through our well-worn frameworks.

The Digital World Opens Doors

The swift changes brought on by the screen age are changing many aspects of human experience—including how and when we talk about faith. This is opening up literal new domains of spiritual conversation.

Relearning Conversation

Speaking of . . . never has listening come at such a premium. Everybody has something to say, and the means to instantly say it to the entire world. *But who is listening?* Those who relearn the sacred art of give-and-take conversation will gain a hearing.

Hospitality as Generosity

It is easier than ever to connect to someone's online profile, but that's no match for connecting with *someone*. Making space for others IRL ("in real life") is increasingly seen as radically generous and countercultural.

Belief Is Multifaceted

It seems like every week there's a new revelation of what brain science is learning about how and why humans believe—and how and why we want to believe. Never before have we understood so much about how faith happens. Due in part to how we're wired, sacred and spiritual experiences—not just information and explanation—are vital parts of the evangelism process.

Longing for Community

People are so isolated. Millennials often feel empty and rejected. Many seek a place to belong based on an activity (like CrossFit) or an interest (like anime). But those bonds aren't strong enough to nurture and sustain a multifaceted human being created in God's image.

Season of Reckoning

Long-hidden systemic sins such as racism, misogyny, sexual abuse and financial exploitation are being brought into the light, and many churches are taking meaningful (and often painful) steps to repent and to heal the wounds.

Culture at the Crossroads

In our research in Europe and elsewhere in the post-Christian West, Barna keeps finding evidence of faith that's flourishing in unexpected places. Breakneck culture change is causing many people to reconsider life in Christ.

WHAT'S NEXT FOR EVANGELISM

By David Kinnaman

With contributions from Aly Hawkins, Paul Pastor and Brooke Hempell

I recently took my 14-year-old son to a speech and debate tournament. Listening to his debate coach, the procedures, policies and point system of the tournament—as time-tested and effective as they may be—struck me as anachronistic to the experiential, visual, digital, feelings-based world of Gen Z. As I drove a minivan full of teenagers homeward, I found myself wondering how a speech and debate program might be built from the ground up for today's requirements—for effective rhetoric and persuasion in digital Babylon. What does the art of persuasion look like today? What elements of persuasive activity can be considered timeless and what might need to be reimagined, reinvented and revived?

Let these questions serve as a backdrop as we consider evangelism. In evaluating the findings from this study, here are four realities to consider—four realities that, if we want to work toward a new gospel movement in our day, we must honestly grapple with.

We Need Deeper Convictions

Human nature, both beautiful and broken. God's nature, both loving and holy. Our need for Jesus to save each of us from sin. These things never change, and this study highlights the Christian community's profound need to bolster our confidence that they matter as much today—in our materialistic, accelerated, frenetic, experience- and emotion-driven society—as ever. Among the convictions that require our recommitment is this: Evangelizing others is good and worthy of our time, energy and investment.

To start, we must pass on resilient faith to Christian young people (this is also a form of evangelism), planning especially for the pivot point of the high school and college-age years. The dropout problem is real, and it has a chilling effect on the overall evangelistic environment. It is impossible to exactly trace the impact of lapsed Christians on non-Christians, but sobering to consider the "de-evangelistic" clout of those who leave the faith. Our team at Barna has been documenting and trying to understand the dropout problem for more than a decade, and we become more convinced every day that faith for the next generation must be among the Church's top priorities.

Even after they are committed to sustaining resilient faith, we must persuade (one might even say "evangelize") younger Christians that evangelism is an essential practice of following Jesus. The data show enormous ambivalence among Millennials, in particular, about the calling to share their faith with others. On one hand, nearly all practicing Christians in this age cohort are fervent in their faith and believe knowing Jesus is vital. But on the other, nearly half view the act of evangelism—sharing about their faith in the hope that another person will come to know Christ—as morally wrong.

Cultivating deep, steady, resilient Christian conviction is difficult in a world of "you do you" and "don't criticize anyone's life

Evangelizing others is good and worthy of our time, energy and investment

choices" and emotivism, the feelings-first priority that our culture makes a way of life. As much as ever, evangelism isn't just about saving the unsaved, but reminding ourselves that this stuff matters, that the Bible is trustworthy and that Jesus changes everything.

We're Evangelizing in the Age of Algorithms

Being tethered to these convictions is critical because Christianity is competing today in the age of algorithms, where technology and entertainment create the rituals, experiences and conversions of our day—a concept we call digital Babylon. When algorithms predict who we want to know based on who we already know, there is no substitute for the gospel power of mutuality and faithfulness in relationships. The everyday work of knowing and allowing ourselves to be known by others is, in these Instagram-filtered days, countercultural. Evangelism can thrive in the Screen Age by focusing on hospitality, conversation and discernment.

In a study on habits and attitudes related to generosity, Barna found that Millennials, more than older generations, highly prize hospitality. To make space for others, to welcome them into your life, is understood by many young adults to be the very definition of generous. Increasing isolation and digital exhaustion prompt their strong cravings for analog relationships and warm human connection.

However, hospitality and conversation are not easy. As I've documented in *Good Faith*, evangelicals report high levels of discomfort and suspicion when it comes to outsiders. Here's the unvarnished truth: If "evangelicals" want to live up to the name, that posture won't help. Evangelism is quintessentially relational, a fundamental act of vulnerability and radical openness.

By anchoring to the unchanging truths of scripture and the reality of God, and patiently cultivating relationships of welcome and generosity, we can lean together into realities that *do* change.

That's the practice of cultural discernment. And make no mistake: The layers of change are exponential, orthogonal, unpredictable, complex. The world today is different from the one in which our institutional ways of doing evangelism were born. It is changed, and it continues to change.

That there is nothing new under the sun (Ecc. 1:9) and that God is doing a new thing (Is. 43:19) are *both* true, at the same time. The best way to live together by the sacred rhythms of God is to acknowledge and respond to both sides of the unchanging-changing reality of God's work in the world.

One way to understand what's changing is to be perpetual learners. Stay interested. Stay engaged. See the whole. Cultural discernment is one of the ways we can begin to revive evangelism.

For example, what are the evangelistic implications of understanding the "disenchanted world" of today's society, where most people live as if there is no supernatural reality or transcendent purpose for human life?* Or what about the fact that we live in a distracted age? It's not just about people having countless and increasing options for ways to spend their time; more deeply, it's about changes in what interests and intrigues human beings. If people are more bored than ever (in church and elsewhere), making church more entertaining will not close the attention gap. Wise cultural discernment leads us to slow down, to dig beneath the surface of trends and to connect with hearts and minds, exercising patience as we rethink what it takes to be persuasive.

Having a clear understanding of our particular cultural moment helps us to become more effective evangelists—not because we get

The world today is different from the one in which our institutional ways of doing evangelism were born

---

* Charles Taylor's A Secular Age, *for example, has provided helpful grounding for Barna's research, allowing us to explore concepts like the new moral code and the centrality of self. James K.A. Smith's* How (Not) to Be Secular *is a great primer on Taylor. Other helpful books include* Disruptive Witness *by Alan Noble and* Strange Days *by Mark Sayers.*

more clever and strategic but, rather that, in telling others about Jesus, we become more reliant on the God who doesn't change but is always up to new things. Aslan is on the move. And we get the privilege of following where he leads.

Here's one comparison of the past with the current cultural moment. In the past:

- Society was less respectful of the individual, even dehumanizing, treating people as expendable. The gospel response was, "Society may not value you, but God does."

- Personal morality was a virtue and people experienced guilt due to moral failures. The gospel response was, "Jesus covers your guilt."

- People's needs were great; government provisions were minimal. The gospel response was to care for the needy through generosity and, in that way, gain a hearing for God's good news.

In the post-Christian culture of today:

- More than ever, society works to uphold human dignity, providing protection for individuals. (Ironically, the Christian community's response is often to focus on whether our own rights are upheld.)

- Citizens of the nation hold fewer moral values in common; social shame is often reserved for beliefs and behaviors that, not very long ago, were considered morally good. Some Christians' response is to shame the shamers; others just try to keep their heads down.

- Society values generosity and charity; governments provide a more robust safety net. Many churches still meet the needs of marginalized people, but struggle against perceptions that they have ulterior motives.

And yet . . . people's need for Jesus hasn't changed. Many people today are missing a sense of *purpose* and *meaning*. People are asking deep questions of identity. *Who am I? What does it mean to be human?* Reviving evangelism will require a gospel response to these kinds of questions.

Our message of new life in Christ must connect to the inner yearnings for abundance, forgiveness, purpose, meaning, relationship and so on. That connection is where the best questions are asked, and where the truest answers are found. If we hope to share the good news in such a way that people can actually receive it, we must have a gospel response to what's happening *now*.

Here's another way to think of it: Cultural discernment is a new apologetics. We learn to connect Jesus to the reality of life today. This is not only being "trend wise," but also being soft and sensitive to the leading of the Holy Spirit, who forms our efforts to know the times and gives us ears to hear what the Lord is saying.

Becoming radically relational, culturally discerning learners will equip us to swim against the all-pervasive algorithmic current.

We Must Get Better at Conversation

No longer can we assume there are just a few loose informational threads to tie up before people trust Jesus. Many Americans—especially young adults and teens—do not have a basic grasp on biblical themes, share a Christian worldview or retain even a rudimentary mental sketch of the gospel. On top of that, in these "post-truth" and "fake news" times, they don't know who to trust.

As the data show, some of us tend to underestimate the part

If we hope to share the good news in such a way that people can actually receive it, we must have a gospel response to what's happening now

that evidence plays in the minds of non-Christians who might consider following Christ. The word itself may conjure up images of textbook apologetics resources, but before we make assumptions about what *all* non-Christians need to know, let's engage individual people. Rather than preparing hyperlinked answers to "frequently asked questions," let's find out what kind of evidence the person in front of us would find compelling. What does he or she mean by "evidence"? Have they gone looking for it and come up empty? What assumptions are behind their desire for it? What need would "evidence" satisfy in their spiritual lives?

Here's an example. "Were Adam and Eve real people?" is an interesting question that is worthy of a good answer. But is there a more profound and consequential question that lies behind my friend asking it? Rather than assuming all they are looking for is "evidence," I could try to find out if there is a deeper question the person wants to ask—maybe about the Creator's intentions for humanity or his purpose for their own life. These are gospel questions, and asking them leads to the true Answer.

If we took time to listen, to get clear on the unanswered spiritual questions that our neighbors, friends, colleagues and fellow speech and debate parents are carrying around—how would our evangelism efforts change? At the very least, we'd become better listeners and more convinced that talking about Jesus is worthy of inclusion in our everyday conversations with others.

Christianity Is True *and* Good

More than ever, we're convinced that people don't just need to be convinced that Christianity is true, but also that it's good—good for their own lives in the real world; good for their neighbors; good for society. Faith-sharing takes place within a specific social and spiritual ecosystem. Like it or not, Christianity's overall reputation in our wider culture intersects with our local and personal efforts to live and share the gospel. This was as true in the first century as it is today. The disruptive ethic of the Jesus community—proclaiming "Jesus is Lord (and Caesar is not)," teaching slave owners to treat their slaves as brothers, and so on—gave Christianity a reputation that was the backdrop of all their evangelistic encounters.

Especially in a 24-hour media context where the words and actions of well-known Christians are seen and heard at all hours of the day, it is naïve to think evangelism happens in a vacuum. In this sense, Christians are not the ones doing the witnessing; everyone else is. And many today don't like what they see.

It's genuinely great that most lapsed Christians and non-Christians like and respect the Christians they personally know. But it doesn't change the fact that many don't feel the same way about "Christianity" as a part of their everyday reality—and we need to be culturally savvy enough to recognize and admit it. Everything Christians do is evangelism or de-vangelism.

Somehow we must live in the tension between reconciling ourselves with our poor reputation and trying to change it. On one hand, there's not a lot any one of us can do to change an entire culture's perceptions; yet the Great Commission remains. We don't get a pass on proclaiming Jesus just because some brothers and sisters make it trickier for the rest of us. It is what it is.

On the other hand, we must set and keep high standards for our families, our churches and ourselves. Integrity is nonnegotiable. The way we repair our collective reputation is by being and doing good, faithfully and over the long term. We know Christianity is true; we must show that it is good. To be clear, we don't earn God's favor or our salvation through good works—grace abounds. Yet our faith in Jesus means we also believe God created us to do good works, bringing glory to God in the process (see Eph. 2:8–10).

Many Christians already take this effort to heart. Against the grain of popular sentiment, our team keeps uncovering evidence

Christianity's overall reputation in our wider culture intersects with our local and personal efforts to live and share the gospel

that many Christ-followers are a force for good in the world. In just the past year, we've found signs in the realms of work, relationships and caring for marginalized and underserved people. For example, three-quarters of practicing Christians strongly agree that "I want to use my gifts and talents for the of good others"; nine out of 10 say it's important to them that their work "contributes to the greater good of society / the world."[11] In a study of poverty activists, we found that self-identified Christians are more likely to report donating money to charity, to feel personally responsible to end poverty and to make significant consumer lifestyle changes to fight poverty.[12] Among those who regularly attend church, the percentages are even higher.

And in new research among 18- to 29-year-olds, we discovered that highly engaged Christians consistently report greater relational connectedness and satisfaction than non-Christians, and express greater interest in talking with and getting to know people who are different from them.[13] When screens and social media so often isolate young people, this finding also demonstrates that Christianity is good.

Finally, Christians can be people of both truth and goodness by practicing extraordinary prayer. We can revive evangelism only to the extent that we locate ourselves in God's plans and God's reality, through a discipline of prayer.

Take time to pray.

Pray for nonbelievers.

Intercede for the next generation of Christians.

Ask God to show you his heart for the world and for those who do not yet know him. Through the power of the Holy Spirit, keep living Christ's kingdom where you are (even at a speech and debate tournament)—and inviting others to join you. ✳

NOTES

1. Barna, *Gen Z: The Culture, Beliefs and Motivations Shaping the Next Generation* (Ventura, CA: Barna Group, 2018).

2. Tom Layman, "CrossFit as Church? Examining How We Gather," Harvard Divinity School, Nov. 4, 2015. https://hds. harvard.edu/news/2015/11/04/crossfit-church-examining-how-we-gather#

3. These findings will be published in David Kinnaman and Mark Matlock, *Faith for Exiles* (Grand Rapids, MI: Baker Books, 2019).

4. Ellie Violet Bramley, "The People's Yogi: How Adriene Mishler Became a YouTube Phenomenon," *The Guardian*, Sep. 25, 2018. https://www.theguardian.com/lifeandstyle/2018/sep/25/yoga-adriene-mishler-youtube-interview

5. Barna, *Spiritual Conversations in the Digital Age: How Christians' Approach to Sharing Their Faith Has Changed in 25 Years* (Ventura, CA: Barna Group, 2018).

6. David Kinnaman and Gabe Lyons, *Good Faith: Being a Christian When Society Thinks You're Irrelevant or Extreme* (Grand Rapids, MI: Baker Books, 2016), 42.

7. Barna, *Spiritual Conversations*.

8. Barna, *Gen Z*.

9. Kinnaman and Lyons, *Good Faith*.

10. Barna, *Christians Who Make a Difference: The Unexpected Connections Between Spiritual Growth and Caring for People in Poverty* (Ventura, CA: Barna Group, 2018).

11. Barna, *Christians At Work: Examining the Intersection of Calling and Career* (Ventura, CA: Barna Group, 2018).

12. Barna, *Christians Who Make a Difference*.

13. David Kinnaman and Mark Matlock, *Faith for Exiles*.

METHODOLOGY

Research for this study included two nationally representative studies of US adults. The first was conducted using an online panel May 8–17, 2018, with 992 practicing Christians. In order to qualify, respondents had to self-identify as "Christian," have attended a church service at least once in the past month and say their religious faith is very important in their life today. A similar study was conducted online with a nationally representative study of 1,001 US adults who do not meet the criteria for practicing Christians. Both lapsed Christians and non-Christians were interviewed.

Both studies have margin of error of ±3 percent at the 95-percent confidence level. Respondents were invited from a randomly selected group of people matching the demographics of the US population for maximum representation. Researchers set quotas to obtain a minimum readable sample by a variety of demographic factors and then minimally weighted the data by ethnicity, education and gender to reflect their natural presence in the known population, using US Census Bureau data for comparison.

ACKNOWLEDGEMENTS

Barna Group wishes to thank our partners at Alpha USA, especially Craig Springer, Todd Proctor, Angela Chadwick, Dane Sanders and David Thomas. What a joy to team up with you to equip the Church to share the gospel!

Many thanks also to our wise and generous contributors, without whose experience and insights this report would be considerably less useful to those doing the everyday good work of sharing faith and equipping others to do the same: Josh Chen, Mary Healy, Michelle Jones, Tim Keller, Kevin Palau and Rufus Smith.

The research team for *Reviving Evangelism* is Brooke Hempell, Pam Jacob, Susan Mettes, Daniel Copeland and Aly Hawkins. Under the editorial direction of Roxanne Stone, Paul Pastor and Aly Hawkins created this report. David Kinnaman and Brooke Hempell contributed additional analysis and insights. Doug Brown edited the manuscript. Roxanne Stone and Aly Hawkins developed the data visualizations, which were, along with the report, designed by Chaz Russo. Brenda Usery managed production with project management assistance from Jennifer Hamel and Mallory Holt.

The *Reviving Evangelism* team wishes to thank our Barna colleagues Amy Brands, Bill Denzel, Cory Maxwell-Coghlan, Raven Hinson, Traci Hochmuth, Pam Jacob, Savannah Kimberlin, Steve McBeth, Jess Villa, Todd White and Alyce Youngblood.

ABOUT THE PROJECT PARTNERS

Barna Group is a research firm dedicated to providing actionable insights on faith and culture, with a particular focus on the Christian church. In its 35-year history, Barna has conducted more than one million interviews in the course of hundreds of studies, and has become a go-to source for organizations that want to better understand a complex and changing world from a faith perspective.

Barna's clients and partners include a broad range of academic institutions, churches, nonprofits and businesses, such as Alpha, the Templeton Foundation, Fuller Seminary, the Bill and Melinda Gates Foundation, Maclellan Foundation, DreamWorks Animation, Focus Features, Habitat for Humanity, The Navigators, NBC-Universal, the ONE Campaign, Paramount Pictures, the Salvation Army, Walden Media, Sony and World Vision. The firm's studies are frequently quoted by major media outlets such as *The Economist*, BBC, CNN, *USA Today*, the *Wall Street Journal*, Fox News, Huffington Post, *The New York Times* and the *Los Angeles Times*.

www.Barna.com

Alpha's mission is to equip and serve the Church in its mission to help people discover and develop a relationship with Jesus. For over 30 years, we've seen Alpha work as an effective, easy-to-use program across every major denomination, culture and context. Alpha is a 10-week course that creates space for people who might not call themselves Christians to ask questions, to explore life and the Christian faith. Alpha creates a friendly, judgment-free environment for people to hear the gospel and process through their doubts. More than a course, Alpha is an idea that creates a deep culture of hospitality, listening, prayer and invitation throughout a church.

Alpha USA comes alongside churches to train, support and provide effective resources for local leaders to run Alpha. In the United States, Alpha runs in over 6,000 churches and 480 prisons, with close to 350,000 participants hearing about the love of Jesus Christ in 2017.

www.AlphaUSA.org

Go and Tell—But How?

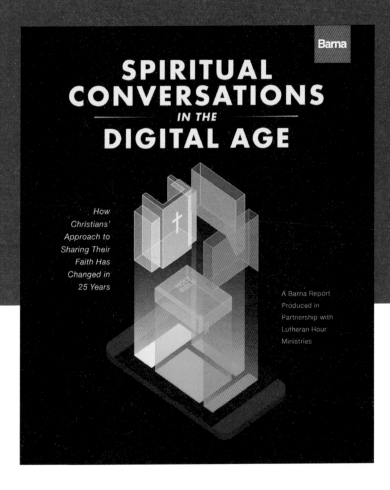

SPIRITUAL CONVERSATIONS IN THE DIGITAL AGE

How Christians' Approach to Sharing Their Faith Has Changed in 25 Years

Barna

A Barna Report Produced in Partnership with Lutheran Hour Ministries

You will learn:

- How priorities and practices have shifted over the past 25 years, including the impact of social media
- Perceptions of faith sharing from both sides of the conversation—the sharer and the hearer
- A data-based profile of eager evangelists
- Generational analysis of today's climate for spiritual conversations

How is our screen-driven society changing the way people talk about their faith? What are the emotions and feelings that people experience when they have these conversations? And what can we learn from those Christians who are most active in sharing their faith with others?

This research will help churches come alongside believers and empower them with confidence to talk about their faith. In doing so, we hope to see Christians begin to make the connections between their everyday, ordinary life and the faith that sustains them. And to tell others the good news of Jesus.

Learn more at
**barna.com/
spiritualconversations**